Dyslexia and Design
& Technology

BDA Curriculum Series
Series Editors: Lindsay Peer and Gavin Reid

Other titles in this series

Introduction to Dyslexia
Lindsay Peer and Gavin Reid
1-85346-964-5

Dyslexia and Drama
Helen Eadon
1-84312-048-8

Dyslexia and English
Elizabeth Turner and Jayne Pughe
1-85346-967-X

Dyslexia and Foreign Language Learning
Gaining Success in an Inclusive Context
Margaret Crombie and Elke Schneider
1-85346-966-1

Dyslexia and General Science
Vicky Hunter
1-84312-050-X

Dyslexia and History
Richard Dargie
1-84312-014-3

Dyslexia and Maths
Julie Kay and Dorian Yeo
1-85346-965-3

Dyslexia and Music
Jane Kirk
1-84312-047-X

Dyslexia and Physical Education
Madeleine Portwood
1-85346-970-X

Dyslexia and Design & Technology

Frances Ranaldi

David Fulton Publishers

David Fulton Publishers Ltd
The Chiswick Centre, 414 Chiswick High Road, London W4 5TF

www.fultonpublishers.co.uk

First published in Great Britain in 2003 by David Fulton Publishers
10 9 8 7 6 5 4 3 2 1

Note: The right of Frances Ranaldi to be identified as the author of this work has been asserted by her in accordance with the Copyright, Designs and Patents Act 1988.

David Fulton Publishers is a division of Granada Learning Limited, part of the Granada plc.

British Library Cataloguing in Publication Data
A catalogue record for this book is available from the British Library.

ISBN 1 84312 015 1

Typeset by Pantek Arts Ltd, Maidstone, Kent
Printed and bound in Great Britain

Contents

Foreword

We are delighted to write the foreword for this book. Frances Ranaldi, in this book, not only describes how the design technology classroom and curriculum can be made dyslexia-friendly, but also highlights how the subject of design technology has progressed in recent years. This is important because, as the author states, many students with dyslexia have natural abilities in this area but are thwarted by the literacy elements of the subject.

Frances Ranaldi also provides some insights into dyslexia itself – the research and the underlying difficulties, since most of the readers of this book may have little knowledge of dyslexia. The whole emphasis of the book is positive. The book is a result of research conducted by the author, as well as her own experiences as a teacher and her personal experiences as a dyslexic person going through school, teacher training and classroom practice.

The book is therefore well equipped with examples including the completion of a portfolio, checklists for subject teachers, strategies for the classroom and workshop, the use of the multiple intelligences model and mind-mapping in the design & technology classroom. The book also has a number of case studies that highlight the pupils' strengths and the type of support required for students with dyslexia. Frances Ranaldi also, through the use of excellent illustrations, shows how design technology can be made user-friendly for the student with dyslexia. The author summarises the key issues discussed in this book in the concluding chapter.

Frances Ranaldi sums up the importance of this book very well when she says that

> this subject offers very real and exciting, positive opportunities … for change to take place. The curriculum of Design Technology can help to produce an environment where a pupil's self-esteem is raised and where they can achieve positive results from their work. It may even encourage the development of future innovative designers, craftsmen and engineers who would have otherwise slipped through the educational net.

This in fact touches not only on the very essence of this book, but indeed on the rationale behind the Dyslexia and Inclusion series of which this book is a part. We hope, therefore, that this book will be widely accepted and appreciated by all involved in teaching design, technology and craft subjects.

Lindsay Peer CBE
Gavin Reid
September 2003

Acknowledgements

The author would like to thank the following people and establishments for their support and contribution towards this book and also for their constant encouragement which was, and is still given towards her as a dyslexia student and teacher:

Mrs Isabella Goscombe
Bill Foreman
Peter Barret
Perth and Kinross Children's Services Department
Kinross High School
Edinburgh University, Faculty of Education, Moray House

Overview of Design & Technology and Dyslexia

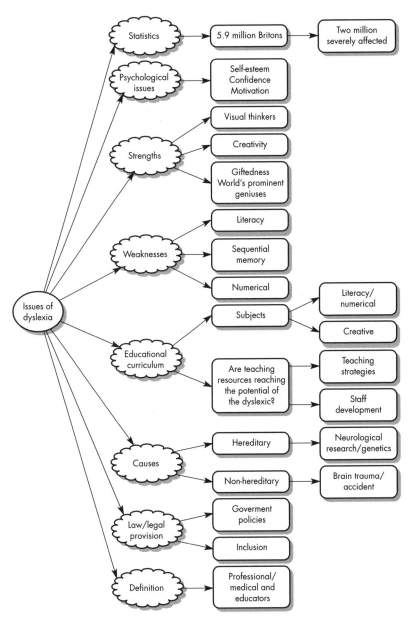

Chapter 1

The Design Technology Curriculum

Design Technology is a subject that has undergone dramatic changes over the past 15–20 years. These changes have made a significant impact on the dyslexic person and other learners who require some form of differentiation. The changes were based on the belief that the introduction of a *design-led* syllabus could result in the raising of pupils' attainments, and also enhance students awareness of career possibilities in a design industry. No longer was Design Technology to be perceived as only a practical craft skills subject, intended mainly for pupils who would pursue apprenticeships in a manual trade. Indeed, the recession throughout the United Kingdom during the 1980s had a dramatic effect on the number of these apprenticeships available. There was, therefore, a need to raise the profile of the subject of Design Technology in schools in order to meet the new demands of industry.

Design Technology can be seen as a creative and a practical subject. This applies to all levels of the examination system and, in order to understand the impact that dyslexia can have on a learner in Design Technology, it is useful to understand the rationale of the curriculum and the challenges it can set for both learners and teachers today.

The Design Technology curriculum

Although the Design Technology curriculum differs between Scotland and the rest of the United Kingdom, the reasons for the change and adaptation of the courses have the same background.

One of the main changes and challenges within the syllabus of craft and design was to introduce a design-led course. This concentrated on exploring the design process from the initial conception of an idea through to the completion of the manufactured product. The courses which pupils can sit involve a combination of practical craft skills and a knowledge and understanding of the design processes, including the appropriate theory for the applications of manufacturing methods and theory required for use of materials and tools.

England and Wales curriculum exams for presentation	Scottish curriculum exams for presentation
ELC Entry level certificate **GCSE** A* – G level **VGCSE** A* – G level **GNVQ – National Vocational** – to be fazed out and replaced by VGCSE qualifications **AS Level** – (= ¹⁄₂ A level) A – E **A level** – A – E	**Access courses** **Standard grade** Credit level – grade 1 & 2 General level – grade 3 & 4 Foundation – grade 5 & 7 **Practical craft skills** **Intermediate 1** **Intermediate 2** **Higher** **Advanced Higher**

It is important to understand the historical background to Design Technology in order to see how much the subject has progressed over the last two decades. One of the individuals who was involved in Scotland with this huge transition over the years is Peter Barret, programme coordinator of the BEd (Hons) Design Technology in Education at Moray House, Edinburgh University. He gives an insight into why changes happened and what is the current reality of Design Technology and differentiation of learning within the curriculum.

Reasons for change of direction

When did the change take place within the subject?
The subject has undergone quite a transition from 1977 to 2003 throughout the United Kingdom. In 1977 the curriculum was called (and concentrated on) Practical Craft Skills and the 1980s saw the development of new qualifications which created an opportunity for change. In 1986, England, Wales and Ireland introduced the GCSEs followed by the introduction in Scotland of Standard Grades in 1987. The introduction of these new syllabuses provided an opportunity to create a Design Technology curriculum.

Why was it felt necessary to introduce new elements of the course?

It was felt that there were three main areas that could benefit from a change in strategy:

- **Educational benefits**. The introduction of the design process was a very important element of the new course. It gave an opportunity to raise the intellectual status of the subject and encourage the theory and investigation of design and the processes which were involved.
- **Industrial benefits**. Given the growing popularity of design within society and the rapidly progressing field of design in industry, it was felt that it would be very beneficial to start the educational process in school where processes and techniques could be learnt and then developed in higher education on design degrees. The skills learnt both in a practical and theoretical nature were being used in the 'real' world, and were considered to be relevant in industry.
- **Equal opportunities**. There has been a very positive encouragement from 1987 to recruit female teachers. It is also now possible for individuals who are themselves dyslexic to become teachers.

Transition of change

How difficult was it to bring about the transformation of a subject that was traditionally seen as a practical, skills-based curriculum?

There were changes which were happening within the subject area as a whole: Mechanical Engineering became Technological Studies; Technical Drawing became Graphic Communications; Wood- and Metalwork became Resistant Materials and Craft & Design.

During these changes the introduction of the design process was met with some resistance within schools from staff who had no previous background in design. They suddenly found themselves in a position of curriculum upheaval in their subjects and had to adapt, digest and teach a course whose profile was being raised in a more academic way than previously. This must have been tackled successfully as we now have within our education system some excellent Design Technology departments throughout the UK which embrace the whole design process including the manufacture of craft work. It is when the subjects are presented in a creative and exciting way that they offer the best potential for all learners. It is particularly useful for those pupils with a differentiated learning style, who will benefit from being challenged intellectually and also within their craft skills.

Was there a comparison made with the English/Welsh and Northern Irish curricula for the subject? Who and what were the deciding factors in altering the course in Scotland?
Historically there has been a difference between the Design Technology curriculum of England, Wales and Northern Ireland and that of Scotland. The Scottish system has always been independent and comes under the authority of the SQA (Scottish Qualifications Authority). It is this body that sets the examinations and the standards within them for the whole of Scotland. In the rest of the United Kingdom the examinations and courses are set by various organisations from which schools can choose and which are accredited by the QCA (Qualifications Curriculum and Assessment):

- AQA
- Edexcel Foundation (which joined with Pearson in June 2003)
- OCR

However, despite the difference of examination authorities and the curricula which they all present, there are common areas of study within Graphic Communications, Craft & Design and Technological Studies.

In Scotland there is not an inclusion of food or textile technology in the Design Technology curriculum; these subjects are covered by a different department.

There is an emphasis on the four-year BEd (Hons) course for student teachers to be aware of differentiation within a classroom. This should, hopefully, have a very positive effect for pupils with learning differences within our subject area. Was the department aware that the Scottish Office funded an HMI report, 'Preparing to Teach Literacy' (HMI 2002). This was published in March 2002 and quotes that it was 'An aspect review of initial teacher education: the quality of the preparation of student teachers to teach literacy from pre-school to S2'.

What are your views on the challenges that can arise from the literacy aspects of design technology?
There is a very serious key issue of what should be taught and how to teach it. In England and Wales there is at present an emphasis devoting more time in the curriculum towards literacy and numeracy skills. The subjects within Design Technology provide an excellent context for numeracy and literacy:

- numbers for calculations
- literacy for reading and listening to instructions and also for research.

Relationship with industry

What have been the most positive points in the change of direction for Design Technology?

Schools that have a design led Design Technology department have embraced the positive aspects of the new type of courses, and some of the pupils in these schools have progressed to high-level design careers following higher education design courses offered in many universities in the UK.

The author's personal experience in the design industry has demonstrated to her that the techniques that are used in a pupil's craft and design folio are very relevant to industry. The folio consists of working on:

- briefs
- specifications
- cutting lists
- initial ideas
- evaluations
- concepts
- synthesis of concepts
- working drawings.

All of these are areas upon which pupils now concentrate in their design folio and are common practice within the design industry. Also the curriculum of Graphic Communications is very relevant to industry. Pupils are working with computer-aided design (CAD), computer-aided manufacturing (CAM) and computer-aided graphics (CAG) programs that are currently being used in design studios in industry and architectural companies.

Rising to the challenge of the Design Technology course

In your view are educational authorities and schools maximising the full potential of the curriculum on offer as it was envisaged?

Unfortunately, no they are not. There has been some excellent work by some education authorities; however, many Design Technology departments are simply trying their very best with the resources available. One of the immediate and main issues that appears to be felt by teachers is containing 'problem' pupils or 'difficult' classes.

In order for the subject to make real headway and help students fulfil their potential there is a need for teachers to work together with other Design Technology teachers to consider key issues and common approaches. It is necessary that this should be led by individuals who have expertise and/or successful experience.

From the perspective of initial teacher education, what is the most challenging aspect for pupils and teachers within the CDT curriculum?

Achieving a balance of theory and practice is the most challenging. There is a perceived view that pupils have to spend a lot of time out in the workshop. From our viewpoint, the rise of the subject's practical craft skills is a real concern because although pupils enjoy the practical work they apply no design knowledge and understanding. There is also a difficult issue for Technological Studies, and the biggest concern there is that there is no broader alternative for those pupils who do not have strengths in maths or science. It is no longer possible to sit this exam at foundation level, and this alienates pupils who may actually excel in a more practicaly based technological course. This, therefore, can present a barrier to some students achieving their potential in Design Technology.

Students undergoing initial teacher education

The biggest challenge for student teachers is to be able to teach all four subjects at all levels. If student teachers are coming directly from school to teacher training their experience of craft skills is very limited. There is a great deal of variation between these courses and they present challenges to both the logical and creative sides of our brains.

Government, local authorities and teachers

The biggest challenge of all is how to improve the learning and teaching while we continue to teach the variety of demanding subjects within the Design Technology curriculum across different levels of exams.

The focus will always remain on the *content* of lessons and the knowledge and skills that student teachers and teachers need to have. So much of the teaching time is taken up with managing resources and 'fire-fighting' problems with equipment and materials, and computers that do not work! All of these factors can prevent teachers from addressing pupils' needs. If a class of 20 is working on individual projects, then this should maximise the individual learning experience. However, if this means that there are only two minutes of individual support given in a 50-minute lesson then the quality of learning is very limited. Providing real differentiation for groups of ability levels (let alone individuals) is very difficult. Most teachers would acknowledge the needs of pupils with learning difficulties, and despite an obligation to provide specific help, seen against this background there is little surprise that more is not being done. It is only recently that attention has been drawn by HMI to the equally important needs of the more able pupil and not simply to expect them to do 'more of the same' but on their own. Enhancing the quality and range of their work is also vital.

(Summary of an interview with Peter Barret 2003)

Providing a curriculum, therefore, that is based on the foundations and principles of differentiation is clearly an ideal worth striving for. Without it, the pupils who require these teaching strategies will have difficulty reaching their full potential. The Design Technology curriculum offers great possibilities for creative teaching which will encourage all pupils. In Chapter 3, issues of dyslexia with Craft & Design will be looked at specifically.

For the purpose of this particular book the author is concentrating on Craft & Design/Resistant Materials. This is in no way diminishing the importance or the popularity of Graphic Communications, Textile Technology, Food Technology and Technological Studies. The principles of the teaching strategies which are discussed in the book are applicable to all these areas.

Chapter 2

Dyslexia: The Issues

Issues for those students with dyslexic difficulties – Specific aspects which are likely to present problems for dyslexic students, and why

Researchers have learned that when typical learners succeed, they credit their own efforts for their success. When they fail, they tell themselves to try harder. However, when the dyslexic succeeds, he is likely to attribute his success to luck. When he fails, he simply sees himself as stupid.

(Ryan 1994)

What is dyslexia?

It is not the purpose of this book to explain the enormous complexities of dyslexia in terms of its biological and neurological causes. However, in order to gain an understanding of dyslexia, and, in particular, the notion of dyslexia as a specific learning *difference*, it is necessary to clarify some possible misconceptions about dyslexia and explain a little about the neurological/medical background. Gaining an understanding of dyslexia and the implications it has on the learner has as important role to play when teaching dyslexic pupils, as has creating a positive environment within the school and classroom.

Many people, both within and outside the world of education, particularly if they are not dyslexic themselves, misunderstand the term 'dyslexia'. For many people dyslexia means a difficulty with reading and writing. Given that the word 'dyslexia' comes from the Greek meaning 'difficulty with words', it is understandable that this perception is the norm. However, this does not give a full explanation of the difficulties and strengths associated with dyslexia.

Although there may still be a lack of appreciation of the different perspectives and the various contributory factors to dyslexia, there is, thankfully, increased public awareness of dyslexia. Many celebrities and famous historical figures are now known to have been dyslexic. Acknowledged historical geniuses such as Leonardo da Vinci, Albert Einstein and Thomas Alva Edison, are examples. The symptoms of this learning difference are diverse and the consequences of the condition have a far greater impact on individuals than is generally recognised.

The British Dyslexia Association describes dyslexia as 'a neurological difference with educational implications' (http://81.89.134.99/main/information/education/e01facts.asp). Lindsay Peer's definition of dyslexia encompasses this greater picture:

> Dyslexia is best described as a combination of abilities and difficulties which affect the learning process in one or more of reading, spelling, and sometimes numeracy. Accompanying weaknesses may be identified in areas of speed of processing, short-term memory, sequencing, auditory and/or visual perception, spoken language and motor skills. Some children have outstanding creative skills, others have strong oral skills, yet others have no outstanding talents; they all have strengths. Dyslexia occurs despite normal intellectual ability and conventional teaching; it is independent of socio-economic or language background.
>
> (Peer 2000b)

Over the past two decades a great deal of international research has been undertaken to discover the neurological and emotional effects of dyslexia, which the British Dyslexia Association describes as:

> a difference in the brain area that deals with language. It affects the underlying skills that are needed for learning to read, write and spell. Brain imaging techniques show that dyslexic people process information differently.
>
> (BDA 2003)

It is estimated that 10 per cent of the population has dyslexia to some degree: 6 per cent mild to moderate and the remaining 4 per cent moderate to severe. Within the United Kingdom there are approximately 300,000 pupils with this learning difference (Peer 2000). There is also a common opinion that it is a condition that affects males more than females. According to Crombie there are more dyslexic boys than girls; the ratio is estimated to be around 1:4 (Crombie 1992: 1).

This view, however, is not held by all, and many educational psychologists have not supported this opinion (personal correspondence between the author and educational psychologists, 2003). They suggest that females are better at hiding this learning difference, and as they do not exhibit the same external behavioural symptoms as boys, a false impression is projected. If the female is an *un*diagnosed or a diagnosed dyslexic, it is possible they have more subtle and introverted ways of developing strategies than their male counterparts. It is important to remember, however, that they may not actually be *successful* coping strategies and as a result they may sense anxiety, low self-esteem and unhappiness. Failure to diagnose correctly may well affect them for the rest of their lives.

This view is supported by the International Dyslexia Association (IDA) who suggest that 'dyslexia affects males and females nearly equally, and people from different ethnic and socio-economic backgrounds as well' (International Dyslexia Association 2001: 4).

Neurological background

In this book, the more common *developmental dyslexia* is the focus, as opposed to *acquired dyslexia*. The latter develops after a trauma such as a head injury. Thanks to scientific studies it is now accepted that dyslexia is *not* a sign of stupidity or low intelligence, although it is possible for people of low intelligence to be dyslexic. There is in fact a genetic cause for the symptoms people exhibit, and in many cases it is an inherited condition.

Genetic findings

The neuropsychological study of dyslexia has made great strides over the past few decades. The consensus view is that it is a developmental disorder with a basis in the brain and in the genes accounted for by the interaction of genetic and environmental factors, i.e. it is epigenetic. The Human Genome Project in America, which began formally in 1990 and ends in 2003, has carried out extensive studies on genetic research: 'Knowledge about the effects of DNA variations among individuals can lead to revolutionary new ways to diagnose, treat and sometimes prevent the thousands of disorders that affect us' (Human Genome Project 2002).

Scientists have been trying to locate the specific genes that are responsible for developmental dyslexia. Grigorenko (1997) reported that there were distinct components of dyslexia which are linked to chromosomes 6 and 15. Other linkage studies by scientists have confirmed this (Fisher *et al.* 1999; Stein 2000) and also highlighted other possibilities. Naploa-Hemmi's (2001) findings stated that the dominant gene for developmental dyslexia is on chromosome 3. However, the same author also published, in 2000, that there is a locus for dyslexia on the chromosome 15q21–q22 region. There is solid research to back up the genetic linkage to dyslexia; the debate on precisely which genes are responsible is ongoing.

It is clear that this is a complex area. Many genes very likely combine to contribute to an individual's potential for dyslexia. Problems in defining the exact and agreed phenotype continue to elude researchers and new findings are published with regularity.

The discovery that there is a biological causation for developmental dyslexia is indeed a positive move forward, both for practitioners and the individuals concerned, as it allows for a better acceptance of the condition and the development of learning strategies. However, the growing base of medical knowledge on the subject is, perhaps unfortunately, creating a negative impression of dyslexia. Dyslexia is usually described as a *disadvantage* to the individual; even the official diagnosis classifies the person as having a disability. Dr Firth of the Institute of Cognitive Neuroscience, University College London, raises the question: 'Is dyslexia based on a specified *brain abnormality* or is it merely part of a continuum of atypical brain development?' Whatever the answer, it is generally accepted that there is a variation from the 'norm' is some way; unfortunately this is usually described or portrayed as a negative deficit. It is estimated that we each have around 30,000–100,000 genes and it is the variation within these genes that makes us unique. Would it not therefore be more logical and positive to consider the view that as individual humans we naturally have different brain compositions (by which the author means how our brains are wired), and that we therefore develop different learning styles, all of which can work, but in different ways.

Despite the often considerable difficulties encountered by dyslexic learners, they also have great strengths. Indeed, the author Tom West (1991) highlights that the strengths within dyslexic people have been invaluable to the progression of society throughout our history. If these strengths are not nurtured or encouraged it would be a great loss to us all. Many of our greatest inventions have been developed by people with so-called 'abnormal dyslexic brains'.

On the surface it would seem feasible to agree with the hypothesis that difficulties for the dyslexic person have become apparent due to the increasing need for a literate society. However, as the condition is not simply linked to literacy skills, and does for example include short-term memory problems or sequencing difficulties, some disadvantages will always be apparent. There is very little research data available concerning dyslexia in pre-literate societies.

The reality of dyslexia is that it is a learning difference. It is important that educators find a positive way to help pupils achieve their full potential and access the curriculum as they deserve to: this must be considered the norm.

The significance of this different learning style

There are undoubtedly some very famous dyslexic people who have achieved great things for themselves. These are success stories that have had a huge impact on society as a whole. Leonardo da Vinci was the original Renaissance man; he was an innovative man of his time, an artist and inventor whose designs we still marvel at hundreds of years later. Without Thomas Edison we would not have the light bulb, gramophones and telegrams, to name but a few of his inventions. Without Michael Faraday we would not have had electricity. He discovered magneto-electric induction, the production of a steady electric current. From his experiments came devices that led to the modern electric motor, generator and transformer.

However, as Peer (2000) pointed out, being dyslexic is not a natural confirmation of a person's high level of intelligence. Despite the success these people have had in their achievements, it would be hard to imagine that any of these high-profile people would *not* have suffered at some point in their lives when coming to terms with the way they learnt things, and with how they expressed their thoughts and theories while learning to develop coping strategies to get them through everyday life. Bruck (1986: 362) suggests that because dyslexia puts children at odds with their environment they can experience great stress, which, in turn, creates many problems for them with regard to their social and emotional adjustment as they mature and become a part of society. It is a recognised fact that the problems which dyslexic learners face on a daily basis can lead to:

- a lack of confidence;
- low self-esteem;
- behaviour issues, which ultimately stem from frustration;
- high levels of stress and anxiety; and
- susceptibility to depression.

> Depression is also a frequent complication of dyslexia. Although most dyslexics are not depressed, children with this kind of learning disability are at higher risk of intense feelings of sorrow or pain. Perhaps because of their low self-esteem, dyslexics are afraid to turn their anger toward their environment and instead turn it towards themselves.
>
> (Ryan 1994)

Trying to explain the feeling of absolute fear, dread and frustration to someone who is not dyslexia, when faced with a situation that exposes them to the very thing their mind won't allow their body to do is incredibly hard. People who are not dyslexic may not appreciate the fear of the 'white out' which may be due to several factors:

- a lack of appreciation that dyslexia is not simply linked to reading and writing;
- very successful avoidance or 'covering-up' strategies employed by the dyslexic learner when faced with a situation or a task that they find hard or impossible to complete.

Adopting a more empathetic manner towards people with learning differences can make a huge impact on the learners' lives. The effects that any learning difference has on an individual should never be underestimated. An educator has both legal and moral responsibilities when teaching all students, and the different learning styles people have must be respected and acknowledged. Lessons should be presented with differentiation as a standard priority within them. Indeed, statute requires local education authorities and their teachers to provide an education that is accessible to all: 'it shall be the duty of authority to secure that the education is directed to the development of the personality, talents and mental and physical abilities of the child or young person to their fullest potential' (Scottish Executive 2000).

In order to create a positive teaching and learning experience for the dyslexic learner and their teachers it is important to understand and to be empathetic to the difficulties faced everyday by dyslexic learners. An extract from Part 3 of the study guide *Dyslexia as a Syndrome: Explanations and Responses* prepared by Reid *et al.* for the Edinburgh University and Open University course for Difficulties in Literacy Development explains these difficulties:

> Wolf and Bowers (2000) suggest that, in addition to their phonological difficulties, dyslexic children process information more slowly. This is the 'double deficit' hypothesis. Fawcett (2002) supports the view that dyslexic children take longer to learn a skill than those who are not:

> Our analysis of how dyslexic children learn (Nicholson and Fawcett 2002) suggests performance can become automatic, but strikingly, our 'square root rule' suggests that this is longer in proportion to the square root of the time normally taken to acquire a skill. So, a skill that normally takes 4 sessions to master would take a dyslexic child 8 sessions, whereas if it normally took 400 sessions, it would take a dyslexic child 8000 sessions!

> (Fawcett 2002: 18)

An American study shows the chemical differences in the brain function of children suffering the learning difference dyslexia. The research, published in the *American Journal of Neuroradiology*, provides new evidence that dyslexia is a brain-based disorder. The interdisciplinary team of University of Washington researchers also showed that dyslexic children use nearly five times the brain area as normal children while performing a simple language task. 'The

13

Controls   Dyslexics

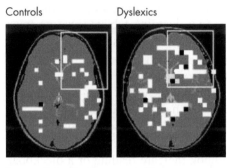

Images show brain areas activated while performing simple language task (white). The grey tone indicates areas activated in two or more children. Pic: Todd Richards, University of Washington

Figure 2.1 Comparison of brain activity

dyslexics were using 4.6 times as much area of the brain to do the same language task as the controls,' said Todd Richards, co-leader of the study. 'This means their brains were working a lot harder and using more energy than the normal children.'

'People often don't see how hard it is for dyslexic children to do a task that others do so effortlessly,' added Virginia Berninger, a professor of educational psychology (http://www.abc.net.au/science/news/stories/s57074.htm).

Figure 2.1 demonstrates that there are clearly different levels and types of brain activity happening between dyslexic and non-dyslexic people and the author feels that this reinforces the idea of Nicholson, Fawcett, Wolf and Bower mentioned earlier.

Below are some of the areas that highlight the variation of difficulties associated with dyslexia.

Possible difficulties
- reading hesitantly;
- misreading, making understanding difficult;
- difficulty with sequences, e.g. getting dates in order;
- poor organisation or time management;
- difficulty organising thoughts clearly;
- erratic spelling;
- processing at speed;
- misunderstanding complicated questions, though knowing the answer;
- finding the holding of a list of instructions in the memory difficult, though able to perform all the tasks;
- remembering people, places and names of objects;
- tiring more quickly than a non-dyslexie person – far greater concentration is required;

- deciphering a passage correctly yet not getting the sense of it;
- great difficulty with figures (e.g. learning tables), reading music or anything which entails interpreting symbols;
- learning foreign languages;
- inconsistent in performance;
- may omit a word or words, or write one twice;
- very likely to suffer from constant nagging uncertainty;
- great difficulty in taking good notes because cannot listen and write at the same time;
- when looking away from a book they are reading or a blackboard from which they are copying, they may have great difficulty in finding their place again;
- works slowly because of difficulties, so is always under pressure of time.

The types of problems experienced in reading might be:
- hesitant and laboured reading, especially out loud;
- omitting or adding extra words;
- reading at a reasonable rate, but with low level of comprehension;
- failure to recognise familiar words;
- missing a line or reading the same line twice;
- losing the place or using a finger or marker to keep the place;
- difficulty in pinpointing the main idea in a passage;
- finding difficulty in using dictionaries, directories and encyclopaedias.

The types of problems experienced in writing might be:
- poor standard of written work compared to oral ability;
- poor handwriting with badly formed letters;
- good handwriting, but production of work is extremely slow;
- badly set out work with spellings crossed out several times;
- words spelled differently in one piece of work;
- difficulty with punctuation and grammar;
- confusion of upper- and lower-case letters;
- writing a great deal but 'loses the thread';
- writing very little but to the point;
- difficulty in taking notes in lessons;
- difficulty in organising work and personal timetable.

The types of problems experienced in mathematics might be:
- difficulty in remembering tables and formulae;
- finding sequencing difficult;

- confusing signs such as + and ×;
- thinking at a high level but needing a calculator to remember basic facts;
- misreading questions which include words;
- confusing directions – left and right;
- finding mental arithmetic difficult, especially at speed.

These may actually have very little to do with understanding mathematics. They are more to do with the underlying dyslexic weaknesses across the curriculum.

Following sequences of operations for a task

Figure 2.2a illustrates the progression of steps within a sequence which are followed in order to complete a task starting at 1 and ending at 10. Figure 2.2b can help to demonstrate the variation in which a dyslexic person may approach the same task. The end result may well be the same; however, the route taken to achieve that result may well be very different with some sequences missed out altogether. The wires within the brain are working at a completely different pace with variations in speed and also creative thinking. It is important to realise and accept that this 'alternative' route may actually lead to a better answer.

> We ought to begin to pay less attention to getting everyone over the same hill using the same path. We may wish to encourage some to take different routes to the same end. Then we might see good reasons for paying careful attention to their descriptions of what they have found. We may wish to follow them some day.
>
> (West 1991)

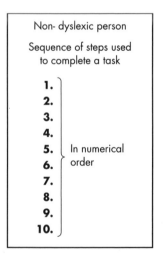
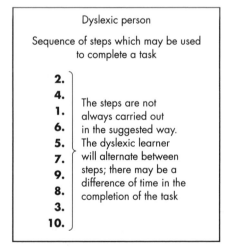

Figure 2.2a, 2.2b A comparison of a sequence of operations between non-dyslexic and dyslexic people

It is clear that there are very real difficulties that may be experienced by the dyslexic learner. These can be as a result of:

- sheer frustration felt at a lack of achievement by a learner;
- misunderstanding the issues involved together with an inadequate perception of the issues involved by teaching staff, the learner's peers and also, sometimes, parents;
- mental and physical exhaustion, which is the result of the concentration that is required by a dyslexic learner in order to perform adequately what appears to others as being sometimes very simple tasks in class.

These issues are often at the root of behavioural problems that can develop in a child causing misery for the learner, their classmates and the teacher. It is also important not to forget the parents or carers of these children who also experience frustration and pain in watching their child become unhappy, withdrawn and sometimes disruptive. It is clearly vital that in order to avoid negative behaviour and experiences in the lives of dyslexic learners that educators find ways of working efficiently with them and their families/carers in order for all to benefit.

> A child who lacks motivation, dyslexic or not, is unlikely to learn much. It is therefore critical that the dyslexic child, who has probably met failure in much of what has been attempted, be presented with material in such a way that errors and failures are minimised and priority given to maximising his success rate.
>
> (Crombie 1992: 47)

Children do not want to be different from their classmates; they want to be doing the same tasks and reading the same stories or texts as their friends. Children as young as primary Yr 1 (or reception in England) are aware of the differences between teaching groups within their classroom and that they can be placed in 'sets' or groups according to their ability. Despite the efforts of the most conscientious teacher in a primary school who concentrates on the whole child and tries to develop his/her strengths positively, the child is still very sensitive to the fact that he/she is 'different' from his/her friends and may be in the bottom group for tasks. This is a very sensitive area for the primary teacher to deal with successfully, and a possible advantage which these teachers have in their favour is the opportunity to know the pupils more holistically.

The approach of education in the primary school is very different from that in the secondary school. In primary school, class teachers have the opportunity of spending more time with the child, understanding individual strengths and weaknesses. In contrast, secondary school pupils are 'on the move' between classes and seeing teachers for as little as an hour a week. It is impossible for mainstream secondary school teachers in specialised subject areas to have the same opportunity for intensive work as their primary colleagues. This understandably makes it difficult to develop teacher–student relationships that are based on an understanding of the individual child's learning style.

Dyslexic people have some very different, but also some extremely positive, qualities which, if encouraged within mainstream education, can enhance their learning skills. If educators were to adopt new teaching methods and, crucially, were provided with practical resources to help these learners, they would also benefit other students. It is a win–win situation. For over a hundred years we have had our schools teaching basically the skills of the medieval clerk – reading, writing, counting and memorising texts. Now it seems we might be on the verge of a new era. In the future we might see the solution of difficult problems in statistics, molecular biology, material developments, or higher mathematics coming from people who are graphic artists, sculptors, craftsmen, film-makers or designers of animated computer graphics. Different kinds of problems and different kinds of tools may require different talents and favour different kinds of brains. The dyslexic brain might well shine in some of these areas.

Learning strategies

There is an increasing awareness in understanding the importance of effective learning strategies in the classroom. Trainers are employed by education authorities to present in-service days which aim to help teachers encourage creative thinking to enhance learning and ultimately benefit industry. From the dyslexic learner's point of view there is a certain irony that one of the methods, which is currently being advocated, is actually an excellent analogy of how a dyslexic mind works. These learners already posses these qualities naturally; they simply need to be allowed to use them.

The non-dyslexic mind tries to develop strategies to allow creative thinking to take place 'off the road'. The dyslexic mind naturally operates there and can experience difficulties in accessing the 'main road'. As Tom West (1991) suggests, we should be paying more attention to the variety of the creative thinking which already exists – and we may actually learn from it.

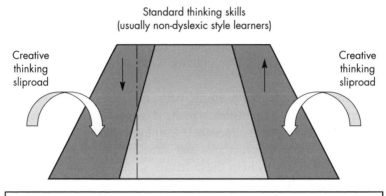

Strategies are used to encourage the more creative side of the brain to 'cross over' the main logical area, which will allow a wider scope of creative thinking to develop and enhance the learning and understanding process.

Figure 2.3 The 'thinking road'

The positive qualities of dyslexic learners

When addressing the Orton Dyslexia Society in 1982, Norman Geshwind, who has studied dyslexia on a neurological level focusing on the advantages of being dyslexic, observes that

> One of the most important lessons to be learned from the genetic study of many diseases in recent years has been that the paradoxically high frequency of certain conditions is explained by the fact that the important advantages conferred on those who carry the predisposition to these conditions may outweigh the obvious dramatic advantages.

In his book *In the Mind's Eye*, Tom West highlights the positive aspects of dyslexia and suggests that if modern science were to cure dyslexia the consequences would be more problematic and would be a great loss to mankind:

> If certain special abilities and dyslexia tend to come together, then in preliterate societies only the advantages would be apparent, not the disadvantages. And, because these conditions have prevailed through most of human history, it is not surprising that dyslexia should be relatively common and would not be evident as a problem until secondary and higher education.

He goes on to explain this in more detail:

> In preliterate societies, these traits would be essential for finding game and shelter in jungles and forests (without maps and signposts). In literate societies, the same traits would be a major disadvantage since its problematic aspects would be more apparent and would lead to major barriers to making meaningful contributions to the society.
>
> (West 1991: 20)

There are many qualities which a dyslexic learner will possess, indeed:

> Graves (1999) suggests that the education system and the employment system waste valuable time concentrating on the weaknesses of dyslexic people rather than their strengths. She suggests that dyslexic people see the overall pattern and grasp sophisticated ideas more easily than simple ones. Additionally, because of their short term memory difficulty they have often to get their ideas down quickly and, being intuitive thinkers, may not be able to explain their thinking process easily to themselves or to others.
>
> (Reid and Kirk 2001)

By viewing the pupil in a more holistic manner it is possible to work with their strengths and weakness much more effectively and ultimately gain a more beneficial and positive learning experience. In order for this to happen we must do more than accept that there are strengths; we must work with the pupils to achieve their full potential. To help learners maximise the benefit from their lesson it is important to realise that dyslexic learners can be:

- innovative thinkers;
- excellent troubleshooters;
- intuitive problem solvers;
- creative in many different ways;
- lateral thinkers.

(Possible strengths – BDA)

Gavin Reid gives a more in-depth description of some of the strengths that dyslexic pupils may have:

- good visual and spatial skills in creative areas such as mathematics, engineering and the physical sciences;
- abilities to recognise patterns in information and to represent three-dimensional images in work with computers;
- a special facility for mentally rearranging designs and information would have a contribution to creative and novel design, as for example, demonstrated by Leonardo da Vinci, Auguste Rodin and Albert Einstein;

- a more holistic way of viewing the world which aids the discovery of problem solutions;
- a rich colour memory and ability to use fast multi-sensorial combinations;
- a willing to meet expectations and have high regard in work;
- good social skills;
- ambitiousness – need to achieve;
- enthusiastic;
- creative;
- good kinesthetic skills [sic];
- critical thinking skills;
- better verbal skills than writing skills.

(Reid and Kirk 2001, Chapter 7)

These acknowledged pointers should give educationalists and authorities the confidence to work and develop teaching strategies which are much more harmonious for the differentiated learner. Examination bodies should also be involved in such a process. It would be very beneficial if these bodies could publicly state that it is acceptable for variations in the presentation of exams and coursework which is submitted to the examination boards. This would give teachers and schools more confidence to be creative in their teaching. Pupils who are trying to jump through the series of hoops in the appropriate manner for both examination boards and the education ministries experience great difficulties unnecessarily.

Legal responsibility

In recent years several acts which have been passed by the government have created groundbreaking effects with regards to inclusion and anti-discrimination. The Special Educational Needs and Disability Act (2001) (SENDA) is particularly relevant; it applies to the whole of the United Kingdom and is being fazed in over a period of four years.

SENDA amended Part 4 of the Disability Discrimination Act 1995 (DDA) to include education. The new Part 4 of the DDA will be implemented in stages:

- the main sections of the Act came into force on 1 September 2002;
- the duty to make adjustments involving auxiliary aids and services (e.g. sign language interpreters, note-takers etc.) came into force on 1 September 2003.

Under the Act, discrimination can occur by treating a disabled person 'less favourably' than someone else for a reason related to their disability, without justification, or by failing to make a reasonable adjustment when they are placed at a substantial disadvantage compared to other people for a reason relating to their disability.

Other important government acts which have influenced a move to a more positive approach to inclusiveness are Children (Scotland) Act 1995; Scotland Act 1998 (*How Inclusive Are Our Schools*), Standards in Schools Scotland Act 2000 (*Improving Our Schools*). These acts have caused a rippling effect within education and have also created opportunities and guidelines for HMI to inspect schools with regards to their ethos and good practice. Schools now have the guidelines from government on what is expected of an 'inclusive school' – social inclusion, equal opportunities, anti-discrimination, cultural recognition, anti-bullying and respect for others.

The government has made a commitment to ensure that there will be an equal and appropriate education for all. The Scottish Executive's Standards in Scotland's Schools Act 2000 is intended to create a statutory framework for schools and authorities to plan, monitor and report on improvements which should be taking place within our education system over the next 3–5 years. '[It] shall be the duty of authority to secure that the education is directed to the development of the personality, talents and mental and physical abilities of the child or young person to their fullest potential (Standards in Schools Scotland Act 2000).

The policy also states a commitment to 'promote equality and help every pupil benefit from education, with particular regard paid to pupils with disabilities and special educational needs'.

The Scottish Executive have pledged over £12 million to fund its new strategies and has introduced a policy which sets out its principles of inclusion and states that in the planning and teaching of the National Curriculum teachers are required to have due regard to the following:

A Setting suitable learning challenges.
B Responding to pupils' diverse learning needs.
C Overcoming potential barriers to learning and assessment for individuals and groups of pupils.

'Applying these principles should keep to a minimum the need for aspects of the National Curriculum to be disapplied for a pupil (Scottish Executive Inclusion policy, p. 1).

It is clear from reading the relevant documents on inclusion that the government is quite specific in its aims of ensuring that the responsibilities given to, and placed with, the teacher (and therefore the local authority) should have due regard to these policies. These very positive proposals and aims envisioned by the policy-makers sound encouraging and promising for the future. However, what is the reality of these proposals? What is actually happening on the ground, within our classrooms on a day-to-day basis, away from the world of politics and academia, which plan and introduce these initiatives?

The 1989 United Nations (UN) Convention on the Rights of the Child and other UN declarations on human rights have influenced the recent changes in Scottish and UK law relating to education and disability. The changes in Scotland's Schools etc. Act 2000 reflects the UN convention principles that all children have a right to education and have their views taken into account when decisions are reached on their education. The Act also reflects international statements on inclusion in that it requires that, wherever possible, children will be educated in mainstream schools. UK disability anti-discrimination legislation has been extended to school education. The Scottish Parliament's Education (Disability Strategies and Pupils' Educational Records) (Scotland) Act 2002 requires local authorities to improve accessibility to school facilities and the curriculum for pupils with disabilities.

The Scottish Executive has stated in its proposals for a draft bill – *Moving Forward! Additional Support for Learning*:

> What is our vision for the future? We wish to see an education system that is inclusive, welcomes diversity and provides an equal opportunity for all children to develop their personality, skills and abilities to their fullest potential.

If an education system is to be all of this, then by welcoming diversity to develop pupils' fullest potential this is truly an opportunity to develop new and diverse teaching and learning strategies for dyslexics and also for others who have different learning requirements. We should be moving away from a narrow view of education which can still permeate within our classrooms – that of 'one glove fits all'. It is impossible to teach a class of pupils successfully using only one method. The issues of staff development and resources will be discussed in Chapters 4 and 5 in more detail; however, as we are looking at the issues faced by dyslexic students at the moment there is a natural overlap.

Chapter 3

Dyslexia and Design Technology: Working Positively

This chapter will consider the subjects which focus mainly on craftwork and design and the knowledge and understanding for these two areas. These areas can be collectively grouped together under the heading of Craft and Design.

Craft and Design

Craft and Design is a subject that is perhaps more traditionally thought of as metalwork, woodwork and plastics. It is a subject that encounters a common perception that pupils really need only to concentrate on practical craft skills and that the outcome of this two-year course will be a coffee table! There are many misconceptions about this particular subject and its course content from many people, including those within education and also from the pupils themselves. It is particularly important that these outdated views are addressed if the true potential of the dyslexic pupil in design technology is to be achieved.

The Department for Education and Skills' description of Design Technology is as follows:

The importance of design and technology

Design and technology prepares pupils to participate in tomorrow's rapidly changing technologies. They learn to think and intervene creatively to improve quality of life. The subject calls for pupils to become autonomous and creative problem-solvers, as individuals and members of a team. They must look for needs, wants and opportunities and respond to them by developing a range of ideas and making products and systems. They combine practical skills with an understanding of aesthetics, social and environmental issues, function and industrial practices. As they do so, they reflect on and evaluate present and past design and technology, its uses and effects. Through design and technology, all pupils can become discriminating and informed users of products, and become innovators.

Curriculum presentations

English/Welsh examination presentations are available from the three main awards bodies OCR (Oxford, Cambridge & RSA Examinations); AQA (Assessment and Qualifications Alliance) and Edexcel:

Resistant Materials Technology *
Textiles Technology
Electronic Products
Food Technology
Graphic Products
Industrial Technology
Systems and Control Technology

*This curriculum is the closest to Craft and Design in Scotland.

Scottish examination presentations available from the SQA (Scottish Qualifications Association):

Craft and Design
Graphic Communications
Practical craft skills – metal
Practical craft skills – wood
Technological studies which consists of:
• Systems Control
• Mechanisms
• Pneumatics
• Energy/work & power
• Structures
• Applied electronics
• Electronic systems
• CAM/CAD

Northern Irish examination presentations available from CCEA (Council for the Curriculum Examinations and Assessment):

GCSE Candidates may work in one or more of the following **focus areas**
Food Technology
Graphic Products
Resistant Materials *
Textiles Technology
Systems and Control

*This curriculum is the closest to Craft and Design in Scotland.

Craft and Design/Resistant Materials

When researching the accessibility of the Craft and Design curriculum the author looked in detail at the first level of formal qualifications from the countries within the United Kingdom. These are:

English/Welsh and Irish – GCSE
Scottish – Standard Grade

If these curricula were not accessible by dyslexic students for the GCSE level or the Standard Grade, it is difficult to imagine that any other awards which follow would be at all achievable, given that they are more difficult. The course content of these courses can be divided into 3 parts:

1. Designing

A portfolio of work on a design project of the pupil's choice detailing written work, design sketches, resources and design solutions which demonstrate a good knowledge and understanding of the design and manufacture process.

2. Practical abilities

A practical piece of craft work as designed and detailed in the portfolio demonstrating a knowledge and understanding of craft techniques and which is graded in respect of the complicity of techniques used, the standard of finish and the independence of the pupil while completing the project.

3. Knowledge and understanding

A minimum of a one-hour written theory exam conducted outside the department in which this external assessment is presented for different levels of ability and for which the pupils are entered for more than one level. This means that pupils can sit two written exams, each lasting for up to two hours.

> Course work, founded on the design brief approach, should underlie all other work in the S3 and S4 and foster independence through a structured and systematic understanding of practical problem solving. A folio of course work should be built up, containing a rich and varied collection of investigative, developmental, research, planning and evaluative material of the candidate's own selection or preparation. In addition, a range of course work artefacts involving a variety of materials should be produced as solutions to design briefs. As part of the course each candidate should design and manufacture a project and produce a related project folio.

> (Course outline. SQA 2002/2003)

The Scottish course outline for Craft and Design is similar to the rest of the United Kingdom where the course title is Resistant Materials, and it is clear from this breakdown that over a period of two years there will be a considerable amount of knowledge and understanding which has to be absorbed and understood by the pupil in order to gain a satisfactory grade in their folio work and written exam. This is no longer a subject which concentrates mainly on practical skills. When taught and learnt effectively and to its full potential, it is a very exciting course. Learning about design should be a stimulating challenge to the pupils. There are many different aspects of design and manufacture to consider and this creative subject can also play a very important role in raising the confidence and motivation of a dyslexic pupil. It is a course that can offer real opportunities for different learning styles and can be taught using the ethos of inclusion and accessibility for all learners whatever their individual styles. There are, however, some barriers for dyslexic learners from the outset which both teachers and pupils need to be aware of. Figure 3.1 demonstrates some of the more obvious barriers which a dyslexic learners will encounter. It is very important to remember that there are wide variations in the symptoms and difficulties which dyslexic learners have, and the pupils are all unique in their overall characteristics. This creates real challenge for educators and education authorities.

There appears to be a general acceptance in society that if a person is dyslexic then they will automatically be a creative person. This assumption is not appropriate. It would be incorrect to assume that *all* dyslexic people are creative. As Peer (2000b) points out, not everyone has an outstanding artistic talent: 'Some children have

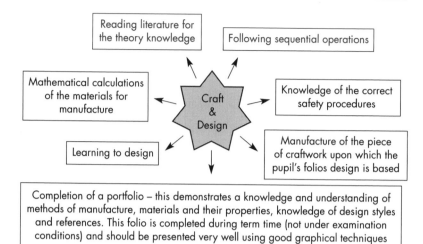

Figure 3.1 Areas within the Craft and Design curriculum which require specific skill and can cause difficulty for dyslexic learners

outstanding creative skills, others have strong oral skills, yet others have no outstanding talents.'

Hornsby considers that dyslexics are on the whole either very good or very bad at using two- and three-dimensional shapes in play or work (1984). However, there does appear to be a high percentage of creative dyslexic people. 'In some art colleges almost a third of the student population are dyslexic and this has considerable implications for support and assessment (The Arts Dyslexia Trust 1996).

A small-scale study by the author in 2002 for a research project in a mainstream Scottish high school (secondary) demonstrated that using figures available from 1997–2002, 61 per cent of students who were diagnosed as dyslexic, or whose learning support record suggested strong dyslexic tendencies, had chosen to take practical and creative subjects. All of the pupils exhibited a combination of problems with reading, writing, numeracy and planning. The statistics were collated from the pupils' non-compulsory subject choices, taken from S3/Key Stage 3 onwards, and the percentage of dyslexic pupils who chose to take a practical craft subject was then calculated. In one standard grade Craft and Design class there were five diagnosed dyslexic pupils, which represented 25 per cent of the class. All five pupils had individual dyslexic characteristics and learning needs.

Learning Support staff	1. An understanding of dyslexia and the support required for equal access to the curriculum.	The departments were extremely supportive of pupils with learning differences. However, they realised they were unaware of how much theoretical work is required by the pupil to pass Craft and Design, and were under the impression that it was a subject that was based mainly on practical skills.
		When a comparison was made of the support given in Art, it was found that there was greater support given to these pupils who required it when writing their essays.
	2. Teaching resources	The departments have no special teaching resources for this subject to help either the pupils or the subject teacher.
Subject teachers	1. An understanding of dyslexia and the support required for equal access to the curriculum.	There was not an awareness of the range of difficulties faced by dyslexic pupils. Their understanding of the condition was limited to reading and writing issues related to dyslexia.
	2. Teaching resources	The departments have no special teaching resources for this subject to help either the pupils or the subject teacher.
Psychologists	1. An understanding of dyslexia and the support required for equal access to the curriculum.	They had an extensive understanding and knowledge of dyslexia and were extremely supportive of the dyslexic pupil. However, as with the learning support staff they were unaware of how much theoretical work is required by the pupil to pass Craft and Design, and were under the impression that it was a subject that was based mainly on practical skills.
	2. Teaching resources	They were unaware of teaching resources specific to this course.

There are misconceptions with regards to the course content of Craft and Design within other school departments, such as guidance and learning support. From discussions with various learning support departments in secondary schools and in educational authorities there appears to be a general consensus by learning support and guidance teachers that practical subjects do not require as much support for pupils with learning differences compared to the more academically perceived subjects. There are several reasons for this none of which are due to to a lack of caring about pupils who needed support:

- a genuine lack of understanding of exactly what the curriculum of Design Technology entails for the learners;
- a lack of communication between departments;
- a lack of resources: the learning support department is continuously stretched to help provide and accommodate for the growing numbers of pupils who require differentiated learning.

Discussions with teaching staff identified two main issues concerning dyslexic pupils and their access to the Craft and Design curriculum: If pupils are not given the correct information about a subject when choosing courses for standard grade at the end of KS2, this will have major consequences for all concerned; and often if a pupil has been diagnosed with dyslexia they are 'persuaded' or 'guided' into taking practical subjects for three main reasons:

1. There is a often a false perception that *all* dyslexics compensate for their 'weaknesses' by having a creative strength.
2. Practical subjects are viewed as presenting the pupils with fewer obstacles. They are viewed as being less academic and therefore pose fewer difficulties.
3. If these pupils take a practical course they are falsely perceived to present less of a demand on the resources of the school's learning support budget, or in some cases from the behavioural support budget.

It is a commonly heard complaint from some Design Technology departments that they are seen as a 'dumping ground' for pupils who are less able or who have behavioural issues.

Problems experienced with course choices for the dyslexic learner

Unfortunately, once the courses have been chosen, pupils not only experience a large jump in the level of work between Key Stage 2 and Key Stage 3 (which is often a more difficult transition for the dyslexic learner compared to their peers), but they also experience difficulties in accessing the information required to pass this, so-called, 'practical' course. This also happens with the transition from Standard Grade to Higher. Still, on the Higher course it is often not until the beginning of the second term of the academic year that the practical craftwork actually begins. Prior to this the time spent is on theory and design planning where there is a requirement for pupils to absorb information and produce work for their folio in accordance with their knowledge and understanding. The written exam paper at the end of the year also requires absorption of knowledge in order to pass it. This external exam tests their knowledge on theory required for designing/planning, materials, methods, applications and an ability to offer critical opinion.

There has been a definite shift in attitude over recent years to raise the confidence of pupils and the status of subjects such as Craft and Design. It is seen as important that such subjects should be a positive experience for the learner. This is particularly important for students with dyslexia as it is a subject in which they can have definite strengths. Therefore, there is an expectation of achieving some personal success in this subject. Yet the difficulties they encounter in the theoretical elements of the course can be a setback to the pupil's confidence. Often they may achieve a top grade for their practical work, showing great aptitude for a subject which may also provide the possibility of a career, but feel thwarted in their efforts because they have not been given the appropriate teaching resources to enable them to revise and pass their written work to the same high standard. This can reduce their grade from a 1 to a 3 or 4. Additionally, this does not give employers, or further education establishments, a true indication of their strengths.

At a glance, it is possible to view these areas that need to be addressed in order for pupils to gain a grade that reflects their full potential. Unfortunately, these are the very areas that can and do create tremendous difficulties for dyslexic pupils. They require skills such as sequencing, reading, writing and revision, all of which may be a cause of stress for pupils, teachers and parents.

Achieving success in teaching an inclusive curriculum depends very much on understanding the pupil and their learning abilities, learning styles and potential. Unfortunately, secondary school may not be particularly conducive to the holistic approach of the individual pupil. Seeing a pupil for a few hours a week cannot possibly allow a teacher the opportunity to get to know all their pupils as well as they might. Indeed, it is not uncommon to take a complete academic year just to begin this progress.

Checklist for subject teachers

- When working with an intake of pupils take note of the confidential notes which are issued by the learning support department on the children in your classes. Be aware of pupils' preferred learning styles.
- Check the appropriateness of textbooks and worksheets. It is important to check if these are appropriate in their layout and interest level, and that they are pitched at a suitable ability level.
- Ensure that pupils have understood the new concept that they are being taught – for example ergonomics or anthropometrics. Often pupils misunderstand the theoretical notions of a new concept as well as the practical applications.
- Encourage other opportunities for pupils to demonstrate their knowledge, apart from writing answers.
- Use a range of multisensory teaching aids: textbooks, story boards, demonstrations and video footage.

If these factors are taken into account then this will result in some clear practical strategies that can help overcome the barriers to learning and create a more positive teaching environment for all pupils and their teachers.

Practical strategies

The notes that are often presented to departments by learning support include all pupils in each year group. The sheer size of this document and the demands on teachers are, unfortunately, off-putting for many classroom teachers. An alternative strategy could be to develop a chart into which your own bank of information on the pupils is added along with any areas that may be of concern specifically for that subject. This is also an opportunity to make notes on the pupil's preferred learning style which will have an effect on teaching strategies used by the classroom teacher. This would also be a valuable teaching aid for a temporary classroom teacher who may be in the department for a period of supply work. An alternative solution would be for the department to utilise the 'new' administrative staffing time…which is now available to bid for within the school, to convert the information on pupils with learning differences to departments and break them down for individual teachers.

An opportunity should be set aside within the department to assess the printed teaching material that is presented to pupils. As resources within departments do tend to be re-used annually, depending on which project is being taught, the initial time spent would have obvious benefits for future years. Within the School Development Plan there is usually an area that focuses on equal access to the curriculum for all pupils. Departments would be justified in asking for developmental time to re-assess their teaching resources, possibly on an in-service teaching day. There is also the possibility of requesting specific development time to be spent with a member of the learning support department to audit the teaching resources currently used in the Design Technology department. This could be a large undertaking which the author does not underestimate. However, developing appropriate levels of teaching resources are vital if dyslexic learners are to have full access to the Design and Technology curriculum.

When assessing whether or not a pupil has understood and absorbed the information and understanding, do not assume that this can only be done in written form. The dyslexic learner may well have strengths in verbal communication; this is a very useful tool to use when in class and also for individual discussions. If a piece of homework has been set to answer particular questions which may come up in the theory exam, allow pupils to have the opportunity to express their knowledge using Mind Maps©, pictorial images and also audio tapes as described in Chapter 4.

There are a number of resources, which can be used while teaching pupils who have a range of abilities (see p. 49–55.) The barriers to using them arise in:

1. Actually creating the teaching resources, and having access to these resources;
2. becoming confident and comfortable in using them as teaching aids; and
3. encouraging the flexible use of a variety of resources within the classroom and giving the pupils the opportunity to become familiar with them to maximise the potential – both of the pupil and the resource.

Allow for short breaks within the class period if the lesson is longer than 40 minutes and theory/design work is the focus of attention.

Work with the learning support department. Ask them for information about appropriate teaching strategies which are specific to the pupils whom they see. When working with pupils on a one-to-one basis or in small groups in learning support departments, do allow for teachers and teaching assistants to offer an insight in which teaching methods specific pupils react with most positively. It is vital that teaching assistants understand the overall view of the Design Technology curriculum as they are often the main support for the pupils.

Strategies for the classroom/workshop

Listed in Chapter 2 are some general areas of difficulty that are experienced by dyslexic learners. It is important to remember that each learner is different and will have a unique combination of strengths and difficulties. Make sure that it is clear to the pupils that you, as a teacher, have high, but achievable, expectations of them.

Strategies for pre-empting difficulties in accessing the literature and information for the subject

- Anticipate that if there are to be any extended pieces of text which have to be read by the pupil, that this information is in the appropriate format and they have the appropriate help.
- Present the information in a non-serif typeface such as Comic Sans or Arial and in a font size no less than 12-point.
- Check if there will be a need for the pupil to write text – either by copying questions and answering them, or when collating revision material.
- Check if there will be an LS member of staff available in class to help the pupil.
- Be aware if the dyslexic learner has a preference for the colour of paper used when writing and printing. The glare that can come from white paper can be extremely problematic for some pupils. They may already have a coloured overlay that they use to help them read textbooks or worksheets.
- Avoid presenting written information on the white/blackboard. This is a very difficult situation for the dyslexic learner and can be a cause of distress. Every time they look up to the board they may lose their place and have to spend valuable time finding it again.

The task will take them much longer than their peers and it will also be more tiring and stressful for them. Even if they manage to write something down, it may not be of any value because they cannot read it back by themselves. Therefore as a piece of information for revision purposes it has very little value. The frustration felt is often expressed by these pupils in one of two ways: either as uncooperative and disruptive behaviour in class, or a retreat within themselves, and by so doing withdraw from the learning process.

- Question whether the process of physically copying down information in rote fashion is actually going to be of benefit to the learning of the pupil. Another strategy may be more effective.

- Be aware that if pupils are to use a scribe in an exam they must have the opportunity of practising this skill long before the examination. It is not as easy as it may appear to explain to someone else what you want to say fluently, and for some children this process at first may be uncomfortable and embarrassing. This will affect performance.

- Provide typewritten notes for pupils – they will have difficulty in taking notes in the classroom. Resources can be transferred on to floppy disks for the pupils to download onto their own PC, or another one in the school. Utilise IT – scan in pieces of text to a computer. Current software now has the facility to read back to the pupil using the increasingly effective 'speak back' function.

- Be flexible and also realistic in the methods adapted for pupils to gather information together. Let pupils use a dictaphone if appropriate. It is possible now to purchase a dictaphone which has a built-in digital camera. This could be a very useful aid for a pupil. They could listen to the discussions and also photograph demonstrations of techniques being presented by the teacher.

- Check regularly that dyslexic pupils have access to relevant information for revision purposes. When a comparison is made between the level of notes taken by a non-dyslexic pupil and a dyslexic pupil there will be a large discrepancy in the quality and volume of course notes taken. If this is the only method available for pupils to revise and learn, the dyslexic learner will be at a significant disadvantage. Expect high standards for the pupils. If appropriate resources are made available to the pupils they should be keeping their notes in good order and up to date. Figure 3.2 demonstrates the discrepancy in suitable revision material.

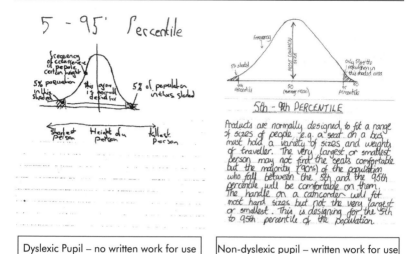

Dyslexic Pupil – no written work for use as revision material	Non-dyslexic pupil – written work for use as revision material

Figure 3.2 Discrepancy in suitable revision material – dyslexic vs non-dyslexic

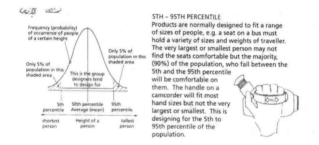

Courtesy of Leckie & Leckie

The two examples shown were written in the same class and with the same time allocation. The dyslexic pupil who produced this work is a hard-working individual who takes great care when trying to copy anything down. He does not draw attention to the fact that he is dyslexic, and because his work is not full of spelling mistakes the fact that he has a learning difference, and is not simply a slow or uninterested pupil, may well be missed. These examples clearly demonstrate the disadvantages dyslexic learners have when trying to collate the required amount of revision material needed to achieve a score for knowledge and understanding which reflects their true potential.

- Involve the pupil, guidance staff and parents in discussions explaining exactly what preparations are being made to allow the pupils access to the curriculum. The involvement of all parties will ensure that there is no communication breakdown. For example, a situation could arise where a reluctant pupil claims to their parents or guardians that they are not receiving the appropriate help in each class. If parents have been included in discussions they will realise that this is not the case. On a legal note, this may prove useful if any action is raised by the pupil against the education authority in the future.
- Provide opportunities for over-learning. Short class discussions at the beginning of the lesson to recap on the last lesson are very beneficial. It is estimated that within one week we will have forgotten 95 per cent of what we learnt the week before.
- If demonstrating a new manufacturing procedure in the workshops keep the instructions simple and logical. Reinforce this with a written set of short instructions on the white/blackboard. If possible, use storyboards which also have models of the procedure.

Multiple intelligences/learning styles

There has been a great deal of research into this area. Furthermore, Howard Gardner claims that all human beings have multiple intelligences that are linked to our learning preferences. These multiple intelligences can be nurtured and strengthened, or ignored and weakened. Gaining an understanding of the different learning preferences that are present within individuals can be a vital piece of the jigsaw when preparing suitable teaching resources for individual pupils. Design Technology is a subject that lends itself very naturally to these intelligences. Practical applications of these intelligences should be explored when teaching pupils, particularly those with learning differences. Gardner believes each individual has eight intelligences. These are explained in Table 3.1 along with the characteristics and Craft & Design strengths. Next to them are the possible situations within the Design Technology curriculum where their use may be appropriate.

Teaching resources should be designed in order to meet the requirements implied by strengths in specific intelligences. This will enable the production of multisensory teaching aids. Education is an

Table 3.1 Gardner's 8 intelligences of the individual

Intelligence type	Characteristics	Craft & Design strengths for dyslexic learners
Visual/spatial intelligence	Puzzle-building, understanding charts and graphs, sketching, painting, creating visual metaphors and analogies (perhaps through the visual arts), manipulating images, constructing, designing practical objects, interpreting visual images	Designing and producing a folio. Designing new concepts
Verbal/linguistic intelligence	Listening, speaking, writing, explaining	Explaining concepts or answers to questions without writing them down
Logical/ mathematical intelligence	Ability to use reason, logic and numbers, performing complex mathematical calculations, working with geometric shapes	Working drawings. Design concepts. This is particularly applicable to Technological Studies
Bodily/ kinaesthetic intelligence	These learners express themselves through movement. Experiencing the physical process of a task enables them to remember and process information	Hands-on experience of practical tasks will provide excellent ways to remember manufacturing processes
Musical/ rhythmic intelligence	Whistling, playing musical instruments, recognising tonal patterns, composing music, remembering melodies, understanding the structure and rhythm of music	When memorising information the use of a poem/rap to do this can help jog the memory in an exam, e.g. a rhyme about the parts on a metal lathe
Interpersonal intelligence	Seeing things from other perspectives (dual-perspective), cooperating with groups, noticing people's moods, motivations and intentions	Designing for specific target markets
Intrapersonal intelligence	These learners try to understand their inner feelings, strengths and weaknesses	Evaluating products, reviewing the specification and the quality of work
Naturalistic intelligence	Studying in a natural setting, learning about how things work. Categorising, preservation and conservation	An affinity with materials. Curious minds for constructional work

ever-evolving process. It would not be a positive move for a teacher to take the introduction of a variety of new teaching aids as a personal insult to the method and style of teaching they may have had over a period of time. This must be viewed logically. There is a biological reason for this learning difference and we are all individuals with individual learning styles.

Case studies

As discussed earlier, dyslexia presents a wide variation of characteristics within the individual. The teaching strategies which are required to enable equal accessibility to the curriculum will vary from pupil to pupil. Below are two case studies for two different pupils with dyslexia, with their reports from primary school. In Scotland the primary curriculum is different from the rest of the United Kingdom and works with the 5–14 syllabus. The reports include comments from subject teachers and both vary in their presentational style.

The levels for 5–14 reporting can be defined below as:

Level A The kind of work most children should be able to do by primary 3
Level B The kind of work which most children can cope with by primary 4
Level C Work which most pupils can cope with by primary 6
Level D Work appropriate for most children by primary 7 (11/12 yrs)
Level E The standard of work which most children could cope with by the end of the second year of secondary school
Level F A high standard which can be achieved by pupils in their second year of secondary school

---

Pupil 1

Chronological age 15 at the time of this report. He is diagnosed as being severely dyslexic. He has a history of behavioural problems which are directly linked to his learning difficulties and the frustration which they cause for him due to a lack of appropriate teaching resources and behaviour management. During his primary education additional class support was given to him after dyslexia was identified.

5–14 report from primary school

Listening level	C	Information handling level	C
Talking level	C	Number, Money & measurement	C

Reading level	B	Shape, position & movement	C
Writing level	B		

Art & design – He enjoys all aspects of this subject and works hard to produce good results.

Drama – He is very imaginative and enthusiastic.

Music – He can read basic musical notations and enjoys playing a variety of instruments.

PE – He works confidently and is enthusiastic.

Environmental studies – He has been very enthusiastic in all the projects and has taken great care with his diagrams, page layouts and charts. His writing is poor, but he understands the need for it and is trying hard.

Personal and social development

He is very friendly and sociable, but is now becoming aware of the social rules of the class and group learning activities. He is always eager to please and responds well to praise. He has enjoyed the responsibility of monitoring duties this session.

In his P6 report it was noted that through oral questioning he showed a good understanding of electrical currents and safety. The class, collectively, had worked on an investigational project and he was able to explain his findings successfully. His Art & Design showed he worked hard.

Secondary school

Pupil 1 has a history of behavioural problems in secondary school. He has not adapted well to the change of environment and teaching styles from primary to secondary school. Within class he can be loud, outspoken very uncooperative with all staff. He makes loud, vulgar remarks concerning other pupils and their family members. He has discipline referrals from several subjects. He shows off in front of his peers.

Age 14 – he has been excluded from school for inappropriate behaviour three times, once throwing an object at a pupil and injuring him.

Subjects which regularly cause difficult behaviour issues for Pupil 1

- Science subjects
- English
- Craft & Design

Discipline measures taken by the school

- detentions
- frequently has lines
- working in the exclusion unit – punching a pupil, disruption, unacceptable language
- referrals to senior management – 'no effort in class, spends a lot of time doing nothing looks for excuses to leave the room. Interrupts frequently.'
- was entered into the Discipline Log of the Craft & Design department.

'He refused to work for a number of lessons. He has interfered with other pupils and is now a threat to the health and safety of the class. He was spoken to repeatedly and offered support. Will be removed to another class with work to do.'

On another occasion he was removed from class as he threw something at a pupil working on the lathe and continued to work out of the workshop for several lessons.

His mother has attended meetings where she admitted that there have been times when she has kept him off school because she feared he would misbehave. She knew that he sometimes behaved in a 'high spirited way'. He annoys members of the local community although he is not in trouble with the police.

Pupil 1 has been involved in these discussions and has been told that he has ability, despite his dyslexia. He is on a behaviour sheet, though this is not proving very effective.

Had direct tuition in S1 twice a week (extracted from history).

It is clear that he spends a lot of effort on avoidance tactics. Teachers report that they feel he uses dyslexia as an excuse and ends up attempting nothing at all in class.

When on his own, without support, he achieves nothing. With support he can achieve the aims of the lesson.

Craft & Design – 'Pupil 1 struggles to achieve any written/drawing tasks. His reading is very poor. His practical craft skills are affected because he cannot measure accurately and read instructions. Behaviour is also a problem because of his difficulties with the class work.'

English – He has excellent listening skills, which he uses to compensate for his reading difficulties. He has a wide vocabulary and good general knowledge. He could make good use of a scribe. He is easily distracted and distracts others.

Maths – He pays little attention and makes little effort even on a one-to-one basis. He works well below his potential.

Science – He is rarely willing to cooperate even from the beginning of the lesson. His recall of facts is very good but he puts little effort into his class work.

Home Economics – His behaviour can be disruptive, but recall is very good.

Modern Studies – As he is a disruptive influence in class he is often removed to work in a small group. He shows some understanding of the subject, but puts little effort into his work.

Learning support

Receives support in English, maths, science, home economics and modern studies. N.B. not Craft & Design. He has a reader and scribe for assessments. However, he cannot read his revision notes back.

There were several incidences of a complete lack of cooperation with the classroom teacher and, on one occasion, deliberate provocation on his part led him to be removed from the classroom. At the beginning of a lesson there were problems when it became clear that the particular subject being taught would involve a little theory – copying some text from the whiteboard. Pupil 1 is aware of his learning differences and appears proud that he can say that Richard Branson and Leonardo da Vinci are, and were, dyslexic. However, he does not seem to grasp the potential of the strengths he has. He is aware of the effects of his behaviour and is very pleased that he can manipulate a situation if he feels that he cannot fulfil a task which is asked of him.

Pupil 1 could be described as the classic dyslexic student, and the very type of personality that many teachers have in their classrooms today. He has difficulty in accepting the fact that he is dyslexic, and is ashamed of his learning difference. His frustration at himself and those trying to teach him manifests itself in his unacceptable behaviour pattern. A very common trait of young dyslexic pupils is their unwillingness to be seen to be different. Is this not a common trait of adolescence? It is very common for dyslexic pupils to avoid, and decline, the offer of an auxiliary member of staff in the classroom to scribe for them as that makes them feel different from the other members of their peer group. Therefore, whatever teaching resources are used, they must be used as sensitively as possible. It is also important that the multisensory methods which are adopted are introduced early in pupils' education so that they become familiar and a normal part of the classroom.

His friends call him 'brainy'. The irony is that he *is* an intelligent child; however, his condition is perceived to affect his intellect.

It is clear that Pupil 1 had a positive experience in primary school where he was educated in a holistic sense. He was able to achieve a sense of success and satisfaction which raised his self-esteem. The abrupt change of atmosphere and environment combined with the anxiety of adolescence upon entering secondary school certainly had a negative effect on him. Dyslexic students require structure and the feeling of security in their environment if they are to reach their full potential. Indeed, that can easily be said of all people whatever their learning style.

Strengths of Pupil 1

Unlike many dyslexic learners he has exceptionally good memory recall and relies on this – and only this – for any revision he needs in order to sit a test. He has excellent recall of a demonstration in metal welding a year previously.

When using IT he presents his work at a high standard. He uses the software to produce a Mind Map© explaining his thought process for his design project. Prior to using this technique, he either failed to do any work on this section of the folio or he asked his classmates to do parts for him. He was very pleased with the results of his work using appropriate techniques.

He clearly has good creative and innovative thinking processes which should be maximised in order to help him with his learning.

Strategies for success

- The use of a PC when developing folio work. This enables him to present his work effectively and pleases him with good results.
- Use of software for a Mind Map©.
- Re-designed worksheets. Sections of text are word-processed onto the worksheet then he only has to copy the diagrams onto the sheet. Other members of the class also do this, while the remaining pupils do the reverse. This strategy works very well as no-one feels different, and everyone is on task, accomplishing something which they can all do.

- Use of a software package which allows for some interaction on the part of the pupil while he is learning about resistant materials and craft skills. However, this is more successful for some if a speech package is attached to the PC.

Pupil 2

Pupil 2 is from a different secondary school and his case notes are in a different style.

Learning support notes
Chronological age 15 at the time of this report and is diagnosed as a moderate to severe dyslexic. During his primary education additional class support was given to him once his dyslexia was identified.

Notes on 5–14 levels in primary 7 – age 11

Listening level	D	Information handling level	D/E
Talking level	D	Number, money & measurement	D/E
Reading level	E	Shape, position & movement	D/E
Writing level	D		

Art & design – He has a good eye for colour, pattern and design.
Drama – He participates fully.
PE – He has excellent coordination. Good dancer, excellent gymnast, agile and light on feet.

He prefers practical subjects and discussions.
Fife summary of intervention (registering concern).

Strategies employed at primary school

- Direct tuition with Learning Support Teacher for early reading skills + rhyme.
- Structured independent educational programmes for reading, phonics and spelling.
- Spelling strategies (home and school).
- Appropriate pacing/teacher expectations according to area.

Staff involved

- Class teacher
- Learning Support Service
- Head teacher.

Long-term aims

- To increase basic literacy skills.
- To ensure that complete curriculum is accessed at an appropriate cognitive level.
- To ensure that he becomes proficient on the keyboard.
- To ensure that self-esteem and self-expectations are raised.

Entry into secondary school 1999

- His difficulties are very specific to spelling.
- Reading has improved greatly. As he has difficulty in identifying wrongly spelt words, it was decided that a Franklin spellchecker would not be of much help.

S2

- Extracted for one period per week for support with written work.
- Working in a small group.
- Using *Beat Dyslexia* pack he is also given one extra period a week for Art.

At a Parents' Evening his mother expressed regret that the support given to her son will be stopped in S3. Additional time will be given for assessments and probably transcription of English writing paper.

S3 aged 15

- sat a biology exam unaided scored a grade 7.
- had the paper read to him and scored a grade 1–2.

It was stated that assessment should be monitored to ascertain the benefit of a reader in certain subjects.

Overview

It is clear that this pupil requires additional help in understanding written questions. He has good ability in reading and this could mistakenly lead people to believe that he is not dyslexic but, instead, a pupil who does not pay attention or is of low intelligence.

Positive strengths

[notes taken from observations of the pupil and discussions with him]

Pupil 2 had a successful and supportive primary school education. His learning difference was detected early on and he was given support from both school and home. He is a quiet natured young man who enjoys, and is successful in physical education. This no doubt has had an effect on his self-esteem as he has a quiet confidence about him. The benefit of Pupil 2 recognising a strength in himself, is that he sees himself as a 'whole' person and he knows he has both strengths and weaknesses. He tries not to let the weakness get him 'down'.

Strategies used successfully

- As with Pupil 1, re-designed worksheets. The sections of text were word-processed onto the worksheet, he only had to copy the diagrams instead. Other members of the class also did this, while the remaining pupils did the reverse. This strategy worked very well as no-one felt different to their peers and *everyone* was on task accomplishing something which they all could do.
- Use of a dictionary in Craft & Design as described in Chapter 4.
- The use of a scribe in class when theory lessons were planned in advance for Craft & Design and also for his examinations. The extra practice of working with a scribe was very beneficial. He was relaxed and was able to express his thoughts well, gaining very good marks.
- Use of videos and software to encourage other methods of over-learning. This worked well and the videos covered the relevant details. He was able to take them home to watch.
- Giving him a sense of responsibility for his own learning and his preferred learning style, e.g. setting tasks from which he could collate information from a variety of different mediums.

  In a research task the class was asked to investigate different styles of chairs by using notes on various styles. Pupil 2 brought in his own sketches, magazine cuttings and a small model of a chair built from cardboard. Although he had far less of his own writing than his class peers, he had brought in appropriate material to demonstrate his findings.
- Use of 'Inspiration' software for MindMaps©.

Summary

The need to have high-quality support for all pupils when they enter education is vital. It is even more crucial if the pupil has a learning difference. Policies on early intervention and appropriate support have been shown to work. From discussions with both pupils, one of the main differences which was observed between them was their levels of self-esteem, one being low and the other secure. This highlights once again that dyslexia is a combination of characteristics which are affected by the environment, and the inner stability of the person concerned.

Difficulties which dyslexic pupils have in gaining the required qualifications to enter further and higher education can prevent them from achievement. Ironically, it is in further and higher education that dyslexic pupils can actually begin to find the best environment for their own style of learning. They have the flexibility of learning in ways which suits them best. This could be in the way they take their notes in a lecture or in the motivation which drives them.

Chapter 4

Teaching Strategies and Resources for Dyslexia and Craft & Design

Teaching strategies

In 1996 Riddick discussed with dyslexic pupils the question 'What makes the "best" and the "worst" teacher?' When this work was published it identified that there are several important factors which contribute towards the 'best' teacher (Riddick 1996: 133). The best teachers:

- encourage and praise;
- help pupils, adapt work and explain clearly;
- understand pupils and do not attempt to humiliate them;
- do not shout;
- have a sense of humour;
- know if children are dyslexic;
- treat all children as if they are intelligent.

The worst teachers:

- are cross, impatient and shout;
- criticise and humiliate pupils;
- are not helpful and are negative about pupils' efforts;
- ignore some pupils and show they consider some pupils 'useless';

- do not understand the problems faced by pupils with difficulties in literacy and are insensitive;
- blame pupils for their problems and call them lazy;
- put red lines through work.

Teachers need to be sympathetic and realistic in their approach and attitude towards learners who need a differentiated curriculum. An appreciation of the cognitive issues involved with dyslexia, together with the working knowledge of appropriate multisensory strategies, which are subject-specific, is crucial.

Strategies for the Design Technology classroom/workshop

Understanding the individual dyslexic pupil

In order to achieve the development and success of an inclusive curriculum it is very important to have an appreciation and understanding of the complex issue of dyslexia and the individuality of pupils' strengths and weaknesses.

The chart overleaf is an adaptation of the information that is sent to all departments from Learning Support in one school. A chart like this can be viewed quickly and also has the flexibility to add in additional notes if there are any strategies or teaching resources which are particularly successful for a dyslexic individual. This is a very useful tool to have both if a new teacher is with the class and to hand on to teachers as pupils progress through school.

Teaching resources

In order to help pupils of all abilities to access the curriculum it is necessary for appropriate multisensory teaching strategies and resources to be included in all our classes as discussed in Chapter 3. This chapter lists some illustrations of variations of teaching strategies which can be used successfully as part of good practice:

- Wherever possible, make sure that information needed for revision is recorded onto an audio cassette.
- Present information on the blackboard carefully.

Even a relatively short piece of text, as shown on p. 51, can cause difficulties for dyslexic learners if not presented appropriately.

Class	Learning difference	Learning style	Strategies/teaching points
Pupil's name			
	Dyslexic		Cannot copy from white/blackboard. Requires printed handouts with bullet points. Requires sequences of operations to be printed with pictorial images of the task. Must be able to use a PC for presentation of written work.
	Dyslexic		Copes well – does not have learning support. Can read texts if in font size 12+. Difficulty with numbers. Very independent and sensitive to receiving obvious help. Requires discreet help.
	Dyslexic/dyspraxic		Motor skills are not strong – needs additional support. Difficulty in copying notes. Very intelligent! Needs challenges which are appropriate to motor skills and mental ability. A wizz with numbers and concepts.
	Dyslexic		Requires teaching notes to be simple and systematic, i.e. simple page layouts of textbooks. Topics covered in textbooks may need to be represented in a new way – additional preparation for teacher.
	ADHD		
	Global learning difficulties		

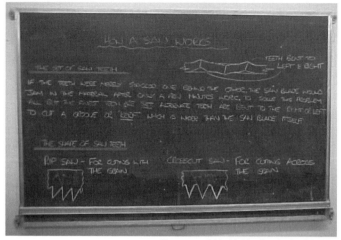

Courtesy of Mr H. Mackaninch, CDT Teacher

Hints for writing on the black/whiteboard

- Avoid writing on the black/whiteboard if possible. If this is the only method available, or favoured by the teacher, then they should arrange for an alternative method for the pupils to collate information. (Pupils are legally entitled to have a copy of the teacher's notes of the lesson.)
- Avoid writing in upper case unless grammatically correct.
- Have information presented on a worksheet where the pupil could draw in the graphics. This will involve the pupil intellectually and they will not fall behind.
- Be sensitive to the difficulties which copying from a board can cause. It may also be the unintended cause of behavioural problems due to frustration at being unable to work at the same pace as their peers.

Personalised dictionary

Looking through a dictionary can be a very stressful experience for a dyslexic person. Some find it difficult to put the letters into the correct sequence within the alphabet, even to find the first letter of the word. This is due to sequencing weaknesses. The whole process is complicated even more if you have little idea how the word is going to be spelt in order to look it up. Confusing? Well, the dictionary can be to a dyslexic learner. It can be a long and frustrating process to accomplish a task which others do with apparent ease.

The introduction of a personalised dictionary may be a useful aid for learners needing differentiation. This could be presented to the class as a whole in the form of a small jotter or in loose sheets which can be put into a binder with tabs for the letter of the alphabet. The main principle of this method is that the new terminology (of which there is a great deal in Design Technology) can be presented in written form to the pupils or written down by them or the scribe. Definitions may be done pictorially to aid the pupil in remembering what the letters in the words mean. The collection of a subject-specific word bank is very useful and allows the dyslexic learner to have the opportunity to practice and revise these new words.

Table 4.1 Descriptions used by dyslexic pupils to help them with revision of words used in CDT

Word	Meaning	Clue
Ergonomics Er go nom ics	The body Surrounding and products used	
Plane (Woodwork) Types: Smoothing Jack	 Finishing wood – smooth it down (smaller size) Larger plane for taking bigger bits off. Think of 'Lumber**jack**' – cutting **big** logs.	

Presentation of tasks

It is vital that in order for any teaching instruction to be successful the tasks be broken down in to 'small, easily assimilated steps'. Figure 4.1 is a worksheet showing the stages in manufacture for a small metal bracket which is part of a craft project. Within the class lesson there is a practical demonstration by the teacher of the steps which are to be followed. No more than 2–3 points at a time are given, leaving time for pupils to complete the first task before continuing with 2–3 more stages. Despite careful planning and care taken by classroom teachers with the demonstration, having a worksheet with the pictorial images laid out in sequence is still very useful for dyslexic pupils (indeed all pupils) to have for their own reference. Although the sheet in Figure 4.1 is well presented, the sequence of operational tasks on the right-hand side may be unclear for a dyslexic learner. There are no numbers for each task and the asymmetrical layout can be confusing for the eye and brain to follow naturally. It needs to be organised in sequential steps for clarity.

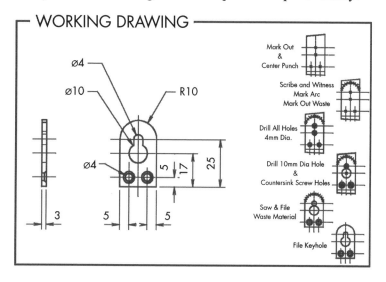

Figure 4.1 Worksheet showing stages of manufacture of a bracket

Flexibility of communication with the teacher

Currently there is a great deal of emphasis from governments and educationalists on the promotion of the 'individuality' of pupils. In order to take this forward into the classroom there must be flexibility regarding the variety of methods which pupils can use to convey their thoughts and knowledge. This is very important in helping a differentiated learner gain confidence in themself and in the subject. Such methods of recording, I believe, should be supported and encouraged by examination authorities if teachers are to have the confidence to encourage this flexibility. Allow for the use of Mind Maps©, pictorial diagrams, and give the the opportunity for pupils to explain verbally. Explanations can also be presented with the aid of IT. There are software packages such

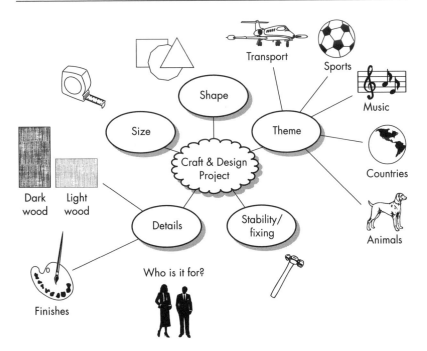

Figure 4.2 Mind Map© layout

as 'Inspiration' which specifically help in designing and presenting Mind Maps© (see Figures 4.2 and 4.3). Written information can be presented with the use of a computer. Answers for set questions can be recorded onto a tape.

Helpful hints for the pupils

Learning is very much a two-way process, and as pupils mature it is important that they begin to take some responsibility for their own learning. In secondary school, the ideal is to encourage pupils to become independent learners. To do this, they will have to adapt to a less holistic approach towards them from the school than they would have experienced at primary level. If pupils are given the encouragement to be more confident about their learning they can take the following steps and discuss the issues with their class teacher.

- Assess whether the typeface used in the book or worksheet is large enough and in an appropriate font style. If not the pupil should be encouraged to indicate this to the teacher and/or Learning Support staff.

- Assess if they can fully comprehend the text that they are reading.
- Build up a dictionary for themselves which may be divided into specific subjects areas. New words, or words which repeatedly cause problems, can be spelt correctly and the description written or drawn in a way that is understood by the individual pupil.
- Establish with which teaching resources they feel they have more positive results, and why? This information needs to be passed on to all teachers.
- Be aware of their own learning style so that they can maximise their strengths in order to tackle the more difficult areas of the curriculum.

Many dyslexic learners have very good coping strategies in place to help them with tasks which they find difficult and which they have had to cope instinctively. However, they may not actually be aware of them or how to maximise them to their full potential.

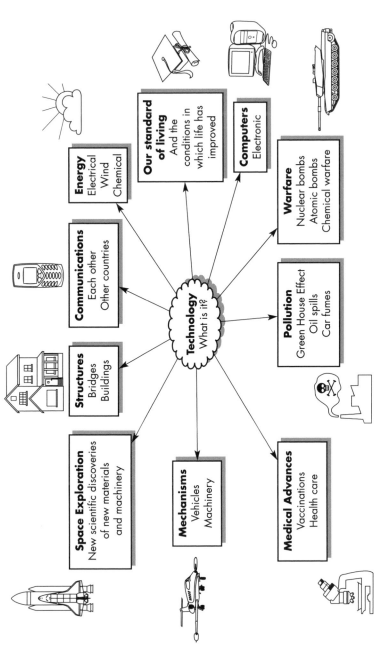

Figure 4.3 The use of pictorial Mind Maps© is very helpful. If software or IT is not available this can be created with printed images cut and pasted onto paper

Chapter 5

Staff Development

Fundamental to the success of inclusion for the dyslexic learner within the Design Technology syllabus (and also to other subjects within the school curriculum) is the issue of staff development and training.

Legal reasons for the justification of staff development

Successive governments have all set out policies which highlight an inclusive education system. Collegiate groups have worked together from many areas of education developing ideas and strategies which have formed legal documents which have been passed through parliaments. In England and Wales, the Department of Education and Skills states that:

> Our aim is to give children an excellent start in education, enable young people to equip themselves with life and work skills, and encourage adults to achieve their full potential through learning.

> (http://www.dfes.gov.uk/index.htm)

The Scottish Executive has stated in its proposals for the draft bill, 'Moving Forward! Additional Support for Learning':

> What is our vision for the future? We wish to see an education system that is inclusive, welcomes diversity and provides an equal opportunity for all children to develop their personality, skills and abilities to their fullest potential.

In Northern Ireland, the key strategic aims of the Department of Education are:

Over the period of the next six years, the Department and its public bodies will seek to achieve the following strategic aims:

- Promotion of Excellence
- Provision of Choice
- Ensuring Equity and Enhancement of Accessibility
- Providing Education and Personal Development for Life
- Doing Things Better

(http://www.deni.gov.uk/about/d_aims.htm)

If the hopes for an education system which encompasses all the aims which governments have set out in the statements above (and in current educational Acts) are to be realised, then it will clearly represent a change in current practice. For example, the new Scottish bill (Moving Forward! Additional Support for Learning) will ensure, more than ever before, that authorities, schools and individual teachers will be charged with the responsibility to provide equal access to the curriculum for all pupils. Cases are now reaching court where education authorities have allegations of negligence raised against them from pupils who have experienced barriers in gaining an equal access to the curriculum. The Phelps v London Borough of Hillingdon case (1997), which reached the House of Lords, is of particular interest because the pupil in question is dyslexic. Following the investigation of this and other cases the court established

the principle that educational psychologists, teachers and other similar staff may be held liable in negligence to the children for whom they are responsible. The court also held that a LEA or school might be 'vicariously' liable for the negligent actions of its staff. This means that an individual could sue an LEA or school if its staff had been negligent.

(http://www.ipsea.org.uk/phelps.htm)

It is now clear that there is a legal responsibility by educational professionals to provide differentiated teaching strategies and resources for students/pupils with disabilities and learning difficulties.

The benefits of staff development

There are several benefits which will develop for an educational authority if they choose to maximise the potential in creating positive, relevant and credible staff development:

- The pupils will benefit;

- The staff – both classroom teachers and support staff – will benefit in their understanding of the issues involved with learning differences, and the presentation of lessons would be more differentiated; and
- They are ensuring that they have provided the appropriate training for their staff in accordance with the current legislation in order to avoid any legal action raised against them in the future from current or ex-pupils. If a teacher chooses not to present differentiated material, despite being trained how to, then there is the possibility that the responsibility may lie with the individual teacher.

Staff development and dyslexia

Quality and relevant staff development in the area of dyslexia should be cross-curricular. It should be aimed not only at learning support staff but also at classroom teachers in order to develop an awareness of learning challenges that pupils who have learning difficulties face daily. Cross-curricular staff development will also present the opportunity to develop and introduce diverse teaching and learning strategies for dyslexics and for pupils with different learning requirements.

The education community should be moving away from an existing narrow view of teaching and learning that can still permeate within our classrooms across the country – the 'one glove fits all' syndrome. It is shortsighted to have the expectation that all the pupils in a class can be taught successfully by taking them all to the same level of attainment using only one method of teaching.

Given that we are all individuals with our own individual learning styles it has always seemed to the author that it is an illogical assumption that humans can all learn in the same way. This view may not be shared by all other educationalists, but those who have different views on teaching and learning will have to be aware of the implications of existing legislation and the 'Moving Forward' draft bill (Scottish Executive 2003). Equal rights already exist within society for learners with a disability or impairment and are protected by the legal system (SENDA 2002; DDA 1995). These rights will be further strengthened. The reality is that even if a teacher is sceptical or cynical in his/her own beliefs regarding differentiation, for whatever reason, these personal views must be put aside, and all teachers have to be given the resources and training in order that they can provide a professional presentation of the curriculum within the letter and the spirit of the equity legislation.

Somehow, within the stresses and demands on the education system and, crucially in the author's opinion, the demands placed upon mainstream classroom teachers, a way forward must be found to allow dyslexic pupils full curriculum access through a national programme. This would benefit both the pupils, as well as the teachers themselves. However, this will only be possible and effective throughout the country if there is funding and opportunities for the key areas of: initial teacher training; continuing staff development; and development of resources to be used within the classroom

Despite government publications and efforts by local authorities, the reality is that equal access to the curriculum for all within schools is still very patchy. This is the situation not only within education authorities, but also within schools and even individual departments. It is clear, therefore, that the government's aims for equal access have not yet permeated through to the classroom and that traditional methods of teaching and learning still prevail. This is despite the very obvious efforts by authorities and some excellent examples of classroom practice throughout the country. Many classroom teachers who may want to develop their knowledge of educational issues and also develop their own teaching resources find themselves hampered by a lack of time. With no centrally, or nationally, developed resources available with learning support for Design Technology, and learning differences, which in this case is dyslexia,

- teachers across the country will either duplicate the time and effort required to produce such resources; or
- will not meet the requirements of current legislation and so limit the very access such resources are intended to promote.

It is important to recognise that there are extremely dedicated teachers in schools who have sympathy for differentiated learners. Unfortunately, the reality is that teachers' timetables are so crowded due to curriculum and assessment commitments that this kind of differentiation, although on their list of priorities, is not ranked too highly because it may simply not be achievable in a practical sense. It is also important to recognise that not everyone is knowledgeable about dyslexia, or indeed other learning differences; nor does everyone possess the passion to address the discrimination which is present within education systems currently and to research alternative solutions. When discussing the subject of inclusion, Peer highlights a very valid point with regards to classroom teachers:

They find themselves in the position of having to possess expertise in a range of areas that were previously not within their remit – and for which in many cases they have no training.

(Peer 2000a)

A teacher may take the view that dyslexia is simply 'another' label or issue which they now have to contend with in the classroom on top of 'everything else'. There is sometimes genuine frustration that new policies and guidelines are introduced by academics who have not actually been practitioners within classrooms for many years, and that they no longer have an understanding of the reality and the stresses which face classroom teachers daily. A number of excellent studies conducted by academics and dyslexic support groups have provided 'good teaching practices' to use when working with differentiated learners and, on a more practical level, some of this research has led to the formation of helpful teaching points as described in Chapter 4. These helpful hints are useful in several ways:

- They enable a teacher to see the wide range of difficulties faced everyday during lessons. Some teachers may not be empathetic or even aware of the difficulties experienced by dyslexic pupils – not because they are unsympathetic, but because they have had no training in the matter, or have no insight into the complexities of dyslexia.
- They encourage teachers to think about developing the different aspects of their lessons in ways they have not done before. This could include presentation methods and the way in which pupils can record their learning.

The research by medical doctors, educational psychologists and specialist teachers has raised a much-needed awareness of this learning difference and has proved that the causes for developmental dyslexia are biological and neurological. It is not, as many people once believed – and as many still believe – that such pupils are simply being lazy or stupid. However, what is now required in order to help pupils and teachers overcome the hurdles faced in the classroom everyday is more practical help. What teachers need and want are positive and workable teaching strategies, which are subject-specific.

If the publicly stated aims of UK governments that they will provide an inclusive and equal education for all learners are to be met, then there must be a major investment to provide relevant and practical resources for teachers to use in the classroom. Although important, it is not enough to provide information simply on the global difficulties faced by dyslexics in general. Staff development that includes practical and relevant information on subject-specific teaching strategies are now required by classroom teachers to enable them to plan their lessons throughout the term.

Within the subject of Design Technology the task of differentiating all the teaching resources within these subject areas for individual schools is enormous, and will never be successful if staff that are very familiar with their subjects, and who have a sound working knowledge of the issues faced in the classroom by differentiated learners, do not carry out the work.

Staff Training

Initial Teacher Education Colleges

These institutions must be the obvious first port of call, and could be ideally positioned to deliver up-to-date, innovative and relevant information regarding all aspects of teaching. There is an enormous opportunity to tap into the enthusiastic and receptive minds of student teachers and to take this unique opportunity to introduce them to the variety of learning differences encountered within our classrooms everyday. Given that there is a legal obligation for *all* teachers to teach literacy within their subject, student teachers of all subjects need to be taught how to address this issue...

> The teacher must have the ability to play his or her full part in developing pupils' skills in literacy.
>
> (SOEID 1998)

> The broad guide lines of the SOIED 1998 are now elaborated in 'Standard for Initial Teacher Education Scotland Benchmark Information 2002'. The key bench mark for ITE in relation to literacy is that student teachers are enabled to acquire the knowledge and understanding to fulfil their responsibilities to meet pupils' learning needs in relation to reading and writing.
>
> (HMI 2002)

Important aspects of literacy

It is important that the definition of literacy is explored and understood by all teachers. For a person to have an acquisition of literacy it means not simply being able to read; it encompasses a wide range of media, some of which can be accessed with greater ease than others by dyslexic pupils:

- reading – access to text from a variety of sources – textbooks, magazines, web pages;
- writing – being able to convey written work in a legible form, either by hand, or computer aided;
- verbal information – information or stories which rely on the spoken word. In some cultures this is the main method used to pass down historical information and techniques on how processes are carried out; and
- pictorial images – these are very much part of literacy – conveying information through graphical representation.

There is, and no doubt will continue to be, great controversy regarding the 'best' method to use when teaching a pupil to read, and it is not the purpose of this book to debate these issues. However, it is important for teachers of all subjects to have some basic understanding of the terminology and methods used when discussing literacy. This is an area that now affects all teachers and not just primary teachers, Learning Support and English teachers, as was once the case. This issue of literacy access has to be addressed through staff development for all teachers in schools, particularly as initial teacher education courses are already very full in terms of content, both in theory and practice.

When the review was carried out by the HMI in 2002 to research how effective the quality of preparation for student teachers to teach literacy is, it was very interesting to note that the only department that was not looked at in the review in any of the teacher training establishments was Design Technology. Given the large amount of literature that has been absorbed by pupils in any of the subject areas within Design Technology, this is an unfortunate oversight. Technological Studies is a highly theoretical subject which includes the use of a great deal of new terminology and requires pupils to understand written information, mathematical calculations and to present their findings appropriately. Student teachers need to be aware of the issues involved.

The role of differentiation within the classroom is taught at college in the global sense, which is very positive. However, what may be missed out is an opportunity to be more specific in the differentiation of the subject content within a school classroom. Given the legal importance of this issue today, it would be very beneficial if there was a module that actually allowed the student teacher to explore different teaching strategies that are suitable for dyslexic pupils across their specific subject and to work with the different curricula available for the subject. A module such as this could be part of a more generic assignment. It could take the form of an investigation which could develop teaching aids that are designed for helping pupils access their subject. This could mean the collaboration of parties with other departments of the faculty, for example those who specialise in equal opportunities, literacy development, special needs and also staff within the student teacher's subject area of the faculty. Other external parties could be: specialist schools, educational psychologists, dyslexic pupils and subject teachers within schools. Providing an opportunity for student teachers to be aware of all the issues involved would enable them to have a far clearer understanding of how they can develop their own teaching to be as inclusive as possible. If they were given the opportunity to explore these issues and also the understanding of the ethical and legal responsibilities during their teacher training, then hopefully this knowledge would remain with them as they begin their actual teaching career. Realistically, it will take a few years for new teachers to begin to feel confident as educators, and it is then when the opportunity to develop differentiation can really take effect within the classroom. If the knowledge from teacher training is still quite memorable then this is a great opportunity to use it.

Looking at the overall course content within a four-year BEd (Hon) in Design Technology in Education course, there must be room for the inclusion of such a module, given that some modules which are taught may not be particularly relevant in their content for the school curriculum and the classroom and may not have the rising legal and equal rights priorities.

A module on Design and Technology and Dyslexia could encompass the following areas:

- an awareness of dyslexia, its causes and its implications;
- What is literacy? Different types of literacy;
- awareness of the literacy debate;
- the legal responsibilities which educational professionals and LEAs have;
- global teaching strategies;
- subject-specific teaching strategies for all the areas of the Design Technology curriculum;
- first-hand experience of pupils with dyslexia;
- visits from, or to, schools that exhibit good practice; and
- the design and manufacture of teaching resources to suit a variety of differentiated learners.

The provision of student teachers with relevant and workable pedagogy and methodology at the start of their careers will eventually filter out throughout the profession, and this good practice will become the norm as new graduates each year become teachers.

Staff development of teachers in schools

Time is a very valuable commodity for the classroom teacher and the lack of it can cause great anxiety. In Scotland, fully registered teachers are now required to spend 35 hours a year out of school on areas of Continuing Professional Development in a suitable and relevant area. (Time spent on individual reading from the up-to-date and relevant journals/research, additional studies or training programmes count towards their CPD.)

Areas to be included in staff development

- an awareness of dyslexia, its causes and the implications;
- the legal responsibilities which educational professionals and LEAs have if this has not already been given by authorities or if the teacher has not recently been taught this during initial teacher training;
- What is literacy? Barriers to literacy and how these can be overcome;
- aims and objectives of their courses – ensuring that the full potential for all pupils could be achieved;
- presentation styles of information;
- information, guidelines and support given to teachers in how to assess their course within the department in order to achieve an inclusive curriculum approach;
- practical teaching strategies which are global and also subject-specific;
- specialised in-service days to tackle these specific issues;
- introduction of subject-specific teaching resources.

As part of an in-service day within school there could be a presentation made to all educational staff in the school regarding the global issues of dyslexia. It is usual within an LEA for one in-service day a year to be spent with all the subject-specific departments in a secondary school attending the same seminar. For example, Perth and Kinross Design Technology departments came together for a planned day, and time within the day was set aside to tackle a particular issue. It could be 5–14 or the Higher Still programmes. Within such a day a presentation could be given on teaching strategies, which are relevant to the subject and also to learning differences. This could also provide an opportunity for teachers to discuss and exchange their thoughts on these issues, and share the successes they will have had in presenting an equal curriculum.

If funding was made available for the central development of resources for differentiated learners, then these in-service days could also be the best opportunity to present them to teachers and demonstrate them working.

Staff can also apply to be released from school to take part in seminars, which are presented outside the school. Seminars on dyslexia are now presented by a range of trainers, both independent and from LEAs, and these are increasingly popular. If the participation from subject-specific teachers increased, then there would be an opportunity for staff attending to disseminate the information to their department. The only negative aspect of these days can be that they tend to be more globally based on the symptoms of dyslexia and general information. They do not tend to be developed for subject-specific teachers who require workable strategies that are relevant to them.

If staff development were to be provided in this way it would ensure that the education authorities' teachers would receive relevant and practical staff development, as opposed to relying on individual teachers to sign up for courses, as the take-up on these would be patchy and could not guarantee that an equal standard of inclusive education is being delivered across the authority.

Areas where staff would appreciate some additional support

A small-scale study in 2002 by the author was taken from different CDT departments in several LEAs. The results showed that the vast majority of CDT teachers were in favour of using alternative teaching resources if they were made available. The main difficulty posed would be in having access to these resources. The teachers were asked the following questions regarding dyslexia and Craft & Design. (Some sections were left unanswered.)

1. **What does dyslexia mean to you, as an individual and as a teacher in mainstream education?**

71%	Difficulty with words and numbers only
14%	Difficulty with words
14%	Requires additional attention from teachers
0%	Difficulties with sequencing

2. **Have you been made aware of the 1995 Disability Discrimination Act and the Special Educational Needs and Disability Act 2002 and their implications?**

71%	No	29%	Yes

3. **Are you, or have you ever been, aware of any difficulties which dyslexic pupils may have in accessing the curriculum?**

28%	No	57%	Yes	14%	only in Teacher Training

4. **Given the pressures of lessons, i.e. the lack of time, resources, management of 20 very different pupils, would you use any teaching resources if they were provided for you (make the assumption that they have been accredited)?**

0%	No	100%	Yes

5. **What kind of teaching resources would you prefer to use?**

Resources	Yes	No	Don't know
Topic-specific storyboards with examples of techniques on them	73%		27%
Audio tapes/CDs on the topics within C&D which the pupils can listen to	71%	14%	14%
Videotapes	71%	14%	14%
Interactive CD-ROM which pupils can use in school and also at home	100%		
Printed material, displayed in a dyslexia friendly layout (this will also be beneficial to many other learners)	100%		
Web page	73%		27%
Other			

6. **Do you feel that there is support from the SQA in this area – alternative presentation techniques being promoted within the folios and exam questions?**

85%	No	15%	Yes

Research: teaching aids for dyslexic pupils

It is vital that research into effective teaching aids and strategies that are subject-specific can take place. The experience of pupils and practising teachers must be taken into account when any specialised programme is developed. This is important as it is the teachers who will use these programmes. Unfortunately, over the years, many resources have been developed across the curriculum and have ended up forgotten, lying in dusty cupboards, because they have become dated or were not really appropriate for the course, the teacher or the pupils.

Craft & Design has a very positive advantage in that the core skills and knowledge that are required for the course are usually the same each year. It would be possible, therefore, to develop a range of teaching resources centrally, which could be distributed to all schools. It is this issue that would be fundamental in creating full access to the Craft & Design curriculum for dyslexic pupils. The central organisation of the development of these resources could take away the difficulties of finance that can very often cloud the issue. These resources should be available to all schools. If a blind pupil is provided with specialist resources which enable their access to a course within the curriculum, why then cannot specialist resources be made available for dyslexic pupils to be used in mainstream education for courses such as Craft & Design? The Disability Discrimination Act 1995 states that a legal responsibility has been placed on education authorities to overcome 'potential barriers to learning and assessment for individuals and groups of pupils'.

Table 5.1 demonstrates that currently there are no specific teaching resources available for Craft & Design to help teachers and dyslexic pupils. Not only were establishments asked, but also commercial companies who specialised in educational aids for dyslexics. The findings were a surprise and, to all concerned, including the pupils, a disappointment.

It is clearly a tall order for education authorities to provide a curriculum which is legally and morally within the realm of equity, but it is important that the fundamental issues of Initial Teacher Education and continuous staff development are addressed in order to make this a reality.

Table 5.1 Are you aware of any teaching aids that have been produced to help dyslexic pupils specifically in the area of Craft & Design?

Establishments	Answer
British Dyslexia Association	[Yes/No]
SQA	[Yes/No]
Dyslexia in Scotland	[Yes/No]
SERC	[Yes/No]
SCREE	[Yes/No]
LEA	[Yes/No]

Chapter 6

Conclusion

To summarise this book would be to highlight the issues involved in providing an equal and accessible curriculum of Design Technology for the learner needing differentiation and who is dyslexic. These issues are relevant to pupils, practitioners, education authorities, governments and parents.

Issues discussed in this book

Background to the subject

This gives a short historical overview of Design Technology and the impact which raising the academic status of a curriculum subject may have on a dyslexic learner in terms of equal access to the course.

Dyslexic difficulties

This explains briefly the medical and genetic reasons for the existence of dyslexia within individuals. Dispelling the myth that it is simply laziness or a lack of intelligence. It also highlights the wide range of characteristics which dyslexic people may have, focusing on both strengths and weaknesses.

Legalities

British and European policies on the equal rights of individuals now encompass education. It is increasingly important that practitioners and education authorities create an accessible curriculum that works in practice and is not simply rhetoric.

Dyslexia in the subject area

Issues in the Craft & Design curriculum are highlighted which may cause difficulty and distress for the dyslexic learner. Areas of strengths which a dyslexic learner may have and which can be tapped into and used positively to access the curriculum are also discussed.

Staff development

It is vital that teachers in specific subject areas are given practical guidance and training in the area of differentiated learning. Using a multisensory approach to teaching and learning benefits not only the dyslexic learner but also the other pupils within the class. This produces a 'win–win' situation for the pupils and their teachers. It is not enough for teachers to have an overview of the characteristics of dyslexia and be given advice in a global sense on how to introduce positive teaching strategies. Subject teachers must be given staff development in order to have an understanding of the areas within their specific subject which affect the dyslexic learner. What will be appropriate for a Language Department, for example, may not be applicable for the subject of Craft & Design. Specific teaching resources will need to be designed and included within the presentation of the course. There are implications for Initial Teacher Training institutions and local authorities to consider when creating and devising courses to suit the requirements of differentiation within an inclusive education system.

Resources

The author is very strong in her belief that specific teaching resources which benefit learners needing differentiation should be available from a central resource accessible by all local authorities and which can be used by all schools. Methods of assessment by examination boards and how they are carried out also need to be addressed to ensure that classroom teachers maximise the ways in which recommendations for assessment may be implemented. Resources which are required for blind and deaf pupils to access the curriculum are available in a way which is not happening for dyslexic pupils. This creates a disadvantage for a section of society who are included under the Disability Discrimination Act. Currently the provision of appropriate multisensory teaching aids is left to the responsibility of the classroom teacher. Given the amount of work which is involved in designing and manufacturing appropriate

71

user-friendly multisensory teaching aids for a whole curriculum, a classroom teacher simply does not have enough time to complete this task along with the other demands he/she has. Therefore these resources should be made available to all. Resources should be made available centrally for research of this kind to take place which will benefit schools on a national level.

In order to achieve a positive learning environment for both teachers and pupils, it is vital that practitioners of education are given the opportunity to understand the complex issue of dyslexia and gain an understanding of the working description which is appropriate to its environment. This must be achieved not only in a global sense but also in the subject-specific sense. Although there is, and no doubt will continue to be, debate within academic circles, there is no doubt that research has categorically shown that developmental dyslexia is the result of certain neurological conditions arising within the formation of the brain. On a positive note, research has demonstrated that if the environmental and behavioural factors which surround a dyslexic individual are taken into account and they are given appropriate support, then a more harmonious and positive learning and teaching environment can be created.

Although dyslexia is classed as a disability and is a specific learning difference, the future for a dyslexic learner does not need to be bleak. One could argue that dyslexia is merely a label which should open doors, securing help and resources which will enable access to an education system which is the same for dyslexic and non-dyslexic learners. It is demoralising for a dyslexic person to be viewed in negative terms, and it can be a traumatic experience coming to terms with this disability. In order to avoid the unnecessary isolation and despondency which dyslexic learners often exhibit, their strengths must be recognised and developed.

It is very much a two-way process – pupils who have continual access to appropriate learning strategies cannot use the label dyslexia as an attention-seeking strategy or as an excuse for not learning. We know the problems are there, and now, thankfully, we understand *why* they are there. Our task is not to lose sight of the importance of the research into dyslexia, or to stop searching for new information, but instead to move on, and create a real change with the knowledge we have.

The subject of this book was Dyslexia and Design & Technology. This subject offers very real and exciting opportunities within these separate subjects for this change to take place. The curriculum of Design Technology can help to produce an environment where a pupil's self-esteem is raised and where they can achieve positive results from their work. It may even encourage the development of future innovative designers, craftsmen and engineers who would have otherwise slipped thought the educational net. Given the importance which societies in all cultures throughout the world attach to modern advancements of technology, aesthetic surroundings and the arts, we should encourage those creative dyslexic learners to achieve.

Resources[1]

There is a vast amount of resources that can be accessed to support students with dyslexia. The following suggestions are a sample of some of these that may be relevant for all age groups, depending on individual literacy and numeracy levels.

Software

1. General principles when choosing software
- Consider the reading and spelling ages and interest levels of the learners.
- Is the learner receiving specialist dyslexia tuition? If so, there may be a program related to, or that will complement, the teaching scheme being used.
- Good software is structured, progressive, cumulative and motivating.
- It is easy for users to find their way around the options in good software.
- Good software is interactive and encourages users to try the tasks.
- It is always best to use programs that have speech support, especially in literacy.
- It is usually best to work through tasks in the suggested program order.
- It is helpful to have software that keeps records of users' progress.

2. Phonic reading and spelling
Wordshark 3. Interactive demo disk available (available from White Space Ltd, 41 Mall Road, London W6 9DG, www.wordshark.co.uk).

---

1. This section first appeared in *Introduction to Dyslexia* by Lindsay Peer and Gavin Reid, published 2003 by David Fulton Publishers. © 2003 Lindsay Peer and Gavin Reid.

It contains the most useful words from all the lists in teaching schemes such as Alpha to Omega and National Literacy High Frequency words at Primary level. Lists can be modified or the student's own words entered. Many alphabet, reading, spelling, sentence- and word-splitting activities with optional difficulty and speed levels in 36 games. Detailed records are kept of the student's progress. This is important as the student, especially students with dyslexia, needs to see that they are actually making progress. This is vital for motivation and self-esteem. Wordshark 3 is designed to run on high-specification PCs and Windows 98 or above. Wordshark 2L is still available for users of older PCs.

The catch-up CD-ROM. Multimedia activities and games to help users learn to read and spell the first 100 high-frequency words using five themed worlds that will appeal to children.

Bangor range of software for Acorn and 4 titles for PC. Different programs with interesting variety for reading and spelling of each level of phonics, based on the Bangor Dyslexia Unit teaching scheme. Some of the programs have a number of ways of reinforcing the words: Chatback; Sounds and Rhymes; Magic E; Soapbox; Punctuate.

3. For spelling mainly

Starspell 2001. The classic 'Look (Hear & Say), Cover, Write and Check' routine with two other activities and optional pictorial support. After practising, a good option is to hear the word without seeing it. Good phonic lists, onset and rime, National Literacy Hour words, a wide range of curriculum vocabulary and context sentences. Own words. Excellent speech. Printable worksheets. Detailed user records.

4. For reinforcement after learning several word families

Gamz Player. A computerised version of their 28 SWAP card games, with a good handbook, quick user guide and other activities. You can customise the sets and enter your own words.

5. Talking books

Hearing the words as you see them makes the experience multi-sensory, which helps dyslexic learners. Users can access the texts at a pace and interest level that suits them, and can follow the text being read.

6. Adventure programs

These may be designed for maths or other subjects, but they also require reading, decision-making, and remembering.

7. Talking encyclopaedias

Masses of information, often with animations, web links and video clips. They are easy to navigate by clicking on internal links. Encyclopaedias without speech can be accessed through text reading software such as textHELP® and Penfriend. The features of textHELP® are read-back speech facility, word prediction – with phonetic and grammar-based predictions, Word Wizard to help search for words and phonetic spellchecker with integrated thesaurus.

8. Word-processors

- Word-processing programs have made a major difference to many dyslexic learners.
- They can help with writing in education, work and leisure activities.
- They can be helpful for supporting the writing process (getting your ideas organised), and also for those who find presentation or handwriting a problem.
- Word-processing is a key written communication tool used in schools, colleges and many work situations.
- Word-processing enables easy drafting and editing. Users can move written text around the page easily, using facilities such as delete, cut, copy and paste. Dyslexic learners don't have to worry about rewriting texts many times over to get a neat piece of writing.
- Word-processed text always looks pleasing. It is easier for their teachers to read too.
- It is particularly helpful in schools and colleges when pupils and students can type longer pieces of work or essays.
- Font size, colour and style can be changed easily.
- Underline, **bold** and *italic* are simple but effective tools.
- Often additional features such as borders, clipart and tables can be added to text.
- It can be useful to use the same word-processing software at home as that used in school or work.
- Some users type very slowly. Using additional wordbanks, grids or predictive programs can help enter text more quickly (see items 12 and 13 below).

9. Talking word-processors

Talking word-processors have a speech facility that enables users to hear the words and sentences as they are being typed. They use synthesised (robotic sounding) speech. This can help accuracy and reassure users that the content makes sense. Many offer a range of voices to choose from. They are used in many schools, especially at KS1, 2 and 3. Some will read toolbars and spellchecking menus, e.g. **Textease**, **Write:OutLoud**. Some talking word-processors have an on-screen wordbank facility.

10. Spellcheckers

Spellcheckers in word-processors can help identify misspellings or typing errors. However, many computer spellcheckers are not very helpful when suggesting a correction list. They usually suggest words that have the first two letters in the spelling error. If these letters are wrong it *may not* suggest the word needed, e.g. type 'sercle' and 'serial' or 'serve' may be the corrections suggested. A hand-held Spellchecker (*Franklin*) may be useful. Talking word-processor, **Write:OutLoud**, incorporates a Franklin Spellchecker. Facilities such as 'search and replace', however, will find repeated errors and correct them. The error (e.g. 'thay') and corrected version ('they') need only be typed once and the other corrections will be done automatically.

11. Quicktionary Reading Pen

Scan a word from any printed text. See the word displayed in large characters. Hear the word read aloud from the built-in speaker or from headphones. Display the definition of the word with one push of a button. Battery-operated (*iANSYST*).

12. Additional on-screen wordbanks and grids

Additional on-screen wordbanks and grids usually have their own speech facility enabling users to hear the words. They can offer multiple lists of words or phrases on screen, for use with the word-processor. Users click on the word or phrase and it is typed automatically into the word-processor. Pictures and recorded speech can be added to some wordbanks. These Wordbanks enable text to be entered quickly and accurately and help users with difficult or subject-specific spellings. Users can create their own grids of words for personal or subject use. The Crick programs have many useful ones ready made for their users, for all key stages that can be downloaded free from their website.

13. Predictive programs

Predictive programs can be used to help cut down keystrokes, save typing time and aid spelling. The program tries to suggest from one or two keystrokes what the user is trying to type from common or regularly used words. It presents the suggestions in a window on the screen where the user can listen and then make the appropriate choice, e.g. type the letter 't' and up to 8 or 9 common words are suggested, such as: 'the, this, there, they', etc. Many of these programs have a speech facility enabling the word-processor to talk (**Penfriend XP, Co:Writer 4000, textHELP!, Read & Write**).

14. Typing and keyboard skills

To make full use of word-processing it is helpful to develop efficient and accurate keyboard and typing skills. There are a number of programs which include keyboard skills.

15. Voice or speech recognition software

Voice or speech recognition software enables users to speak the words they want to word-process. This may be a useful option especially for older pupils, students and adults. However, it may be not as easy as it sounds. It takes time and training.

16. BDA ICT booklets

These booklets are available from the British Dyslexia Association, 98 London Road, Reading RG1 5AU, UK, and are written and presented in a user-friendly manner.

Mathematics

Books

Agnew, M., Barlow, S., Davies, O., Pascal, L., Skidmore, S. (1995) *Get Better Grades with Maths*. London: Piccadilly Press (ISBN 1-85340-392-X).

Chinn, S. J. (1996) *What to Do When You Can't Learn the Times Tables*. Baldock: Egon Publishers. (also available as a CD-ROM *REM*)

Chinn, S. J. (1998) *Sum Hope: Breaking the Numbers Barrier*. London: Souvenir Press.

Chinn, S. J. (1999) *What To Do When You Can't Add and Subtract*. Baldock: Egon Publishers.

Chinn, S. J. and Ashcroft, L. R. (1998) *Mathematics for Dyslexics: A teaching handbook* (2nd edn). London: Whurr.

Miles, T. R. and Miles, E. (eds) (1992) *Dyslexia and Mathematics*. London: Routledge.
Robson, P. (1995) *Maths Dictionary*. Newby Books (ISBN 1-872682-18-4).

Maths study and question books for all key stages

CGP (Tel. 0870 750 1262).
Henderson, A. (1989) *Maths and Dyslexia*. St David's College, Llandudno.
Using ICT to Support Mathematics in Primary Schools (training pack available only to schools). DfES (0845 60 222 60) (Ref. 0260/2000)
IANS: The Informal Assessment of Numeracy Skills.
Available from Mark College (www.markcollege.somerset.sch.uk)

Software for maths

Numbershark-PC. (KS1–3) Numbershark is by the makers of Wordshark and has the same type of colourful, fun graphics in structured learning tasks and a similar range of enjoyable reward games. It covers number recognition and sorting and the four main rules of number, i.e. addition, subtraction, multiplication and division. The actual numbers are represented in the games, as words, in a number-line, as rods, in digits, on an abacus, in a scale, and on a numberpad, which provides variety. Dyslexic pupils who have problems with short-term memory, sequencing skills and short attention span love this software and the 30 different activities. It gives them the chance to build up confidence, and the opportunity to practise and try out those aspects of number that worry them, in an easily accessible way. Study of the manual by the supervising adult is essential as there are so many options.

It is important to choose useful levels and to work through the teaching and practise activities as well as applying them in the games. (White Space Ltd, demo disk available. Tel/Fax: 020 8748 5927; e-mail: sales@wordshark.co.uk; www.wordshark.co.uk)

Maths Circus Act 1. PC, Acorn, Mac (KS1–3) Twelve different games can be played and each one has five levels of difficulty. All the puzzles require reasoning skills. There are straightforward instructions. Players simply press an arrow to work through the different levels of the package. The colourful graphics relate to circus life with seals, lions, high wire acts, etc. A simple colour-coded record is kept of each player's progress. They can log on with their special player code and tackle additional tasks. The early levels can be solved bytrial and error but learners gain the greatest benefit if they verbalise their reasons for following a procedure to solve a puzzle. For teachers there is also a useful set of 24 activity sheets which can be photocopied. There are now Maths Circus Acts 2 & 3 for those who have cracked the first set of puzzles. (4Mation, tel: 01271 325 353; fax: 01271 322 974; e-mail: sales@4mation.co.uk; www.4mation.co.uk)

MathMania PC. Acorn. (KS2–4) Navigate through a maze finding a key and reaching the exit with the required score. Score points by collecting gold bars or by answering questions to get through barriers. Once each maze is completed, a puzzle appears and then another maze. There are four levels of difficulty for the questions, which can be set on number, time, measurement, shape and space or a mixture of all these in a lucky dip. It is possible for teachers to edit the question bank. Pupils enjoy this program as it is simple to use and fits well into a short lesson. The questions vary from simple sums, like 5 + 8, to the equivalent in words. The latter is most useful as this is an area that causes great problems in maths. MathMania is simple and effective and good value. (Topologika Demo download and on CD-ROM, tel: 01326 377 771; fax: 01326 376 755; e-mail: sales@topologika.com; www.topologika.co.uk)

Chefren's Pyramid. (KS3) This will challenge the whole family and this adventure can easily become addictive. You have become separated from your group on a tour of the Pyramids and have to find your own way out, passing through a series of rooms as you go. To move through a room you must answer all its questions correctly. If you make more than one mistake, you are dropped back to the room below! You can save your position to return on another occasion. The questions start with simple single figure addition and move upwards through many different mathematical topics, mostly suitable to KS3 learners. Ideally this program will provide a means for parents to work with their children. For older 'children' there is also Cheop's Pyramid. (Nicholl Education Limited, tel: 01484 860 006; fax: 01484 860 008; e-mail: admin@nicholl.co.uk; www.pyramid-maths.com)

BDA ICT Booklets.
Catch 'em Young (early learners).
Count on Your Computer. Ideas and suggestions for using technology to support maths and numeracy (for all key stages).

Creative writing

Inspiration is a software program to help the student develop ideas and organise thinking. Through the use of diagrams it helps the student comprehend concepts and information. Essentially the use of diagrams can help to make creating and modifying concept maps and ideas easier. The user can also prioritise and rearrange ideas, helping with essay-writing. Inspiration can therefore be used for brainstorming, organising, pre-writing, concept mapping, planning and outlining. There are 35 in-built templates and these can be used for a range of subjects including English, history and science. Dyslexic people often think in pictures rather than words. This technique can be used for note-taking, for remembering information and organising ideas for written work. The inspiration program converts this image into a linear outline. The program is available from: iANSYST Ltd, The White House, 72 Fen Road, Cambridge CB4 1UN (tel: 01223 42 01 01; fax: 01223 42 66 44; e-mail: sales@dyslexic.com) (supply excellent reading and spelling computer programmes suitable for dyslexic students).

Motivation

Start to Finish Books. This series of books (Don Johnston, 18 Clarendon Court, Calver Road, Winwick Quay, Warrington WA2 8QP, tel: 01925 241642; fax: 01925 241745; www.donjohnston.com), can be beneficial as the series, designed to boost reading and comprehension skills, provides a reader profile, a computer book, audio cassette and paperback book. Designed to engage children in reading real literature, the series can help with fluency and motivation. Some of the topics included in the series are: history, famous people, sports, original mysteries and re-tellings of classic literature. Don Johnston also produce some excellent software for children with literacy difficulties. This includes **Write: OutLoud3** (discussed above). This program supports each step of the writing process including: generating ideas – helps with brainstorming and researching topics; expressing ideas – this allows children to hear their words as they write; editing work – using a spellchecker designed to check for phonetic misspellings; revising for meaning – helps with word-finding and improves written expression.

Reading fluency

The Hi-Lo readers from LDA, Cambridge and other similar books, such as those from Barrington Stoke Ltd, 10 Belford Terrace, Edinburgh EH4 3DQ, can be beneficial in relation to motivation. These books, particularly those from Barrington Stoke, have been written with the reluctant reader in mind and they can help students with dyslexia with reading fluency, in maintaining reading comprehension and generally developing processing speed. Barrington Stoke have also a series of books devoted to teenage fiction.

Penfriend. This software, from Design Concept, 30 South Oswald Road, Edinburgh EH9 2HG (tel: 0131 668 2000; www.jasper.co.uk/penfriend) provides an excellent word prediction tool and also has an on-screen keyboard specifically aimed at children with dyslexia and writing difficulties. It also provides three lexicons for different ages, and new word lists for different topics can be created.

Teaching reading

Toe by Toe Multisensory Manual for Teachers and Parents (Keda Cowling, available from Keda Publications, 17 Heatherside, Baildon, West Yorks BD17 5LG, tel: 01274 588278). Toe by Toe is a multisensory teaching method highly recommended for teachers and parents. The programme has a multi-sensory element, a phonic element some focus on the student's memory through the planning and the timing of each of the lessons in the book. It can be used readily by parents and the instructions are very clear.

Stride Ahead – An Aid to Comprehension (Keda Cowling) can be a useful follow-up to Toe by Toe. Essentially, Stride Ahead has been written for children who can read but may have difficulty in understanding what they are reading. (Available from Keda Publications, 17 Heatherside, Baildon, West Yorkshire, BD17 5LG, tel/fax: 01274 588278.)

Interactive Literacy Games (Crossbow Education, 41 Sawpit Lane, Brocton, Stafford ST17 0TE, www.crossboweducation.com). Crossbow Education specialises in games for children with dyslexia and produce activities on literacy, numeracy and study skills. These include 'Spingoes' and onset and rime spinner bingo which comprises a total of 120 games using onset and rime; 'Funics' a practical handbook of activities to help children to recognise and use rhyming words, blend and segment syllables, identify initial phonemes and link sounds to symbols. 'Funics' is produced by Maggie Ford and Anne Tottman and is available from Crossbow Education. Crossbow also produce literacy games including Alphabet Lotto, which focuses on early phonics, 'Bing-Bang-Bong' and 'CVC Spring', which help develop competence in short vowel sounds and 'Deebees', a stick and circle board game to deal with b/d confusion. They also have board games called 'Magic-E', 'Spinit' and 'Hotwords', a five board set for teaching and reinforcing 'h' sounds such as 'wh', 'sh', 'ch', 'th', 'ph', 'gh' and silent 'h'. 'Oh No', a times table photocopiable game book, and 'tens 'n' units', which consists of spinning board games which help children of all ages practise the basics of place value in addition and subtraction.

Staff development

BDA Handbook, published annually by the BDA, 98 London Road, Reading RG1 5AU.

Fawcett, A. (ed.) (2001) *Dyslexia: Theory and Good Practice.* London: Whurr Publishers.

Peer, L. and Reid, G. (eds) (2000) *Multilingualism, Literacy and Dyslexia.* London: David Fulton Publishers.

Peer, L. and Reid, G. (eds) (2001) *Successful Inclusion in the Secondary School.* London: David Fulton Publishers.

Reid, G. (2003) *Dyslexia*: *A Practitioner's Handbook* (3rd edn). Chichester: Wiley.

Reid, G. and Kirk, J. (2001) *Dyslexia in Adults.* Chichester: Wiley.

Reid, G. and Wearmouth, J. (2002) (eds) *Dyslexia and Literacy*: *Theory and Practice.* Chichester: Wiley.

Website links

Adult Dyslexia Organisation
(www.futurenet.co.uk/charity/ado/index.html)
Arts Dyslexia Trust (www.sniffout.net/home/adt)
British Dyslexia Association (www.bda-dyslexia.org.uk/)
Creative Learning Company New Zealand
(www.creativelearningcentre.com)
Dr Gavin Reid (www.gavinreid.co.uk)
Dyslexia Association of Ireland (www.acld-dyslexia.com)

Dyslexia Institute (www.dyslexia-inst.org.uk)

Dyslexia Research Trust (www.dyslexic.org.uk)

Dyslexia in Scotland (www.dyslexia-in-scotland.org)

European Dyslexia Academy for Research and Training E-DART (www.psyk.uu.se/edart/)

Helen Arkell Dyslexia Centre (www.arkellcentre.org.uk)

Hornsby International Dyslexia Centre (www.hornsby.co.uk)

I am dyslexic – a site put together by an 11 year old dyslexic boy – (www.iamdyslexic.com)

Institute for Neuro-Physiological Psychology (INPP) (www.inpp.org.uk)

International Dyslexia Association (IDA) (www.interdys.org)

Learning and Behaviour Charitable Trust New Zealand (www.lbctnz.co.nz)

Mark College (www.markcollege.somerset.sch.uk)

Mind-field (www.mind-field.org)

PATOSS (www.patoss-dyslexia.org)

Quantum Learning (www.trainthebrain.co.uk)

Red Rose School and Dyslexia North West (www.dyslexiacentre.com)

School Daily New Zealand (www.schooldaily.com)

ICT suppliers

iANSYST (www.dyslexic.com)

Crick Software (www.cricksoft.co.uk)

Inclusive Technology (www.inclusive.co.uk)

SEMERC (www.blackcatsoftware.com)

Xavier Educational Software (www.xavier.bangor.ac.uk)

This chapter has provided an overview of some of the resources that may be suitable particularly for the student with dyslexia in the secondary school. Many of these, however, are also appropriate for primary-aged children, but the important point is that age-appropriate materials need to be used for the student in secondary school even if his/her reading age is at a primary level. This can be more motivating for the student and can enhance the possibility of success in each area of the curriculum. It is important to recognise, however, that the barriers to learning experienced by many students with dyslexia can be overcome not only with the use of resources but through teacher and management awareness, curriculum planning and staff development.

Bibliography

Bee, H. (1998) *Lifespan Development* (2nd edn). Harlow: Addison-Wesley Educational Publishers Inc.

British Dyslexia Association (2001) *Achieving Dyslexia Friendly Schools* (2nd edn). Reading: BDA.

British Dyslexia Association (2003) http://81.89.134.99/main/information/adults/a01what.asp.

Bruck, M. (1986) 'Social and emotional adjustment of learning disabled children: a review of the issues', in Ceci, S. (ed.) *Handbook of Cognitive, Social and Neuropsychological Aspects of Learning.* Hillsdale, NJ: Lawrence Erlbaum Associates.

Crombie, M. (1992) *Specific Learning Difficulties (Dyslexia): A Teacher's Guide.* Glasgow: Jordanhill College of Education (ISBN 1 85098 485 9).

Dickinson, C. (2000) *Effective Learning Activities.* Stafford: Network Educational Press (ISBN 1 85539 035 3).

Disability Discrimination Act 1995.

Fawcett, A. J. (2002) 'Dyslexia and literacy: key issues for research', in Reid, G. and Wearmouth, J. (eds) *Dyslexia and Literacy: Theory and Practice.* Chichester: Wiley.

Fisher, S. E., Marlow, A. J., Lamb, J., Maestrini, E., Williams, D. F., Richardson, A. J., Weeks, D. E., Stein, J .F. and Monaco, A. P. (1999) 'A quantitative-trait locus on chromosome 6p influences different aspects of developmental dyslexia'. *American Journal of Human Genetics,* **64**, 146–56.

Given, R. and Reid, G. (1999) *Learning Styles: A Guide for Teachers and Parents.* Red Rose Publications. The foundation for people with learning disabilities.

Grigorento, E. L. (1997) 'Evolution of haplotypes at the DRD2 locus'. *American Journal of Human Genetics,* **57**(b), 1445–56.

HMI (2000) *How Good is Our School? Special Education Needs.*

HMI (2002) *Preparing to Teach Literacy* (ISBN 0 7053 1010 8).

Hornsby, B. (1984) *Overcoming Dyslexia: A Straightforward Guide for Families and Teachers*. Optima (ISBN 0 356 14499 2).

Learning and Teaching Scotland (2000) *5–14 Environmental Studies*. Scotland: Scottish Executive.

Naploa-Hemmi, J. (2000) 'Two translocations of chromosome 15q associated with dyslexia', *Journal of Medical Genetics*, **37**(10), 771–5.

Naploa-Hemmi, J. (2001) 'A dominant gene for developmental dyslexia on chromosome 3', *Journal of Medical Genetics*, **38**(10), 658–64.

Norris, L. and Linton, P. (2000) *Craft & Design Standard Grade Course Notes*. St Andrews: Leckie & Leckie (ISBN 1 898890 85 4).

Peer, L. (2000) *Multilingualise, Literacy and Dyslexia: A Challenge for Educators*. London: David Fulton.

Peer, L. (2000a) *Winning with Dyslexia? A Guide for Secondary Schools* (2nd edn) p. 5. Reading: British Dyslexia Association.

Peer, L. (2000b) 'What is dyslexia?', in Smythe, I. (ed.) *The Dyslexia Handbook 2000*. p. 67. Reading: Bristish Dyslexia Asociation.

Peer, L. (2001) *Handy Hints Poster for Secondary School Teachers*. Reading: British Dyslexia Association.

Peer, L. and Reid, G. (2001) *Dyslexia: Successful Inclusion in the Secondary School*. London: David Fulton Publishers in association with the British Dyslexia Association (ISBN 1 85346 742 1).

Reid, G. and Kirk, J. (2001) *Dyslexia in Adults: Education and Employment*. Chichester: Wiley.

Riddick, B. (1996) *Living with Dyslexia*. London: Routledge.

Ryan, M. (1994) 'Social and emotional problems related to dyslexia', *Perspectives*, **20**(2).

Scottish Executive (1999) *Social Justice: Milestones and Definitions*. Scotland: Crown Copyright.

Scottish Executive (2000) *Standards in Schools Scotland Act 2000*. Scotland: Crown Copyright.

Scottish Executive (2000) *Improving Our Schools: Responses to the Riddell Report*. Scotland: Crown Copyright.

Scottish Executive (2003) *Moving Forward! Additional Support for Learning* (ISBN 0 7559 0691 8).

Scottish Office (1995) Children's (Scotland) Act, 1995. Scotland: Crown Copyright.

Scottish Office (1998) *How Inclusive Are Our Schools?* Scotland Act 1998. New Community Schools Prospectus. Scotland: Crown Copyright.

SOEID (1998) *Guidelines for Initial Teacher Education Programmes in Scotland*. Scotland: Crown Copyright.

SQA (2002/3) *Conditions and Arrangements for National Qualifications*. Scotland: Crown Copyright.

Stein, J. (2000) 'The role of the Magnocellular System.' Keynote address at the Fifth BDA International Conference, York.

West, T. (1991) *In the Mind's Eye.* New York: Prometheus Books (ISBN 0 87975 646 2).

Wolf, M. and Bowers, P. G. (2000) 'The double defecit hypothesis for the developmental dyslexia'. *Journal of Educational Psychology*, **91**, 415–38.

World Health Organisation (1986) Fifth Global Conference on Health Promotion – 'Bridging the Gap' (Ottawa Charter). Mexico City, 5–9 June.

Websites

American Journal of Neuroradiology www.ajnr.org

British Dyslexia Association www.bda-dyslexia.org.uk

Department for Education and Skills (England and Wales) www.dfes.gov.uk/index.htm

Department of Education in Northern Ireland www.deni.gov.uk/about/d_aims.htm

HMI (Crown Copyright) www.hmie.gov.uk

Human Genome Project www.ornl.gov/hgmis/project/about

International Dyslexia Association www.interdys.org/abcsofdyslexia/page4.asp

Learning and Teaching Scotland www.ltscotland.org.uk

Medical research papers www.ncbi.nlm.nih.gov

Office for Standards in Education www.ofsted.gov.uk

Phelps Case Law www.ipsea.org.uk/phelps.htm

Scottish Executive www.scotland.gov.uk/education/newcommunityschools

Times Educational Supplement www.tes.co.uk

Index